A Kind of Passport

NCTE Research Report No. 24

A Kind of Passport

A Basic Writing Adjunct Program and the Challenge of Student Diversity

Anne DiPardo
University of Iowa

National Council of Teachers of English
1111 W. Kenyon Road, Urbana, Illinois 61801-1096

For Mike and Ben

NCTE Stock Number: 25484-3050

Library of Congress Cataloging-in-Publication Data

DiPardo, Anne, 1953–
    A kind of passport: a basic writing adjunct program and the challenge of student diversity/Anne DiPardo.
        p. cm. — (NCTE research report; no. 24; ISSN 0085-3739)
        Originally presented as the author's thesis (Ph. D.)—University of California at Berkeley.
        Includes bibliographical references and index.
        ISBN 0-8141-2548-4
        1. English language—Rhetoric—Study and teaching—Case studies. 2. Minority college students—Social conditions—Case studies. 3. College students—Social conditions—Case studies. 4. Education—Demographic aspects—Case studies. I. Title. II. Series.
    PE 1011.N295 no. 24
    [PE 1404]
    808'.042'07—dc20   2092-41740
                                                                              CIP

Contents

Acknowledgments

If this book speaks to you, chances are it is because of the striking candor of the research participants—students, group leaders, faculty, and administrators—whose voices occupy its most noteworthy moments. As my time in the field drew to a close, my efforts to express appreciation were often flicked aside with selfless disclaimers: "If this can help somebody else, well, then..." I am left with the sense that I still have not adequately thanked those who made this work possible, whose courage and trust inspired me to push past writing blocks and false starts. They gave me a story worth telling; I only hope they find that my telling of it justifies their investment of time and faith.

This research was originally written up as a doctoral dissertation at the University of California at Berkeley, where my mentor and thesis chair, Sarah Warshauer Freedman, provided her usual sage advice and firm encouragement. Sarah's vision and care have richly informed this work and so much else besides; suffice it to say that as I was writing about the need to provide insightful, individualized attention to students, I was abundantly blessed by such attention to my own work. Thanks also to Berkeley professors Guadalupe Valdés and Don McQuade for their readerly feedback on my dissertation manuscript; and to Glynda Hull and Anne Haas Dyson, who offered sensitive response to various drafts of my proposal. The NCTE Research Foundation provided welcome financial assistance, easing the economic pressures of my final year in graduate school.

The task of revising my dissertation for publication was completed during my first year as an assistant professor of English education at the University of Iowa, where colleagues and students have provided opportunities for lively conversation about many of the issues at the center of this report. Iowa City is a long way from "Dover Park," but the support that I have found here has moved me toward new understandings of my work there. Special thanks to Jim Marshall and Mary Beth Hines for valuable suggestions on an earlier draft, as well as for their friendship and good humor.

Finally, thanks to my husband, Mike, for listening, reading, and keeping our preschooler happy while I sat hunched over yet another draft. His support of my work is manifest in multiple ways, only some of which are apparent upon the page.

I Background and Design

Contexts are nested, from the most immediate to the act of speaking to the more distant: classroom, school, school system, community, and so on; and the classroom context is never wholly of the participants' making.

—Courtney Cazden, *Classroom Discourse: The Language of Teaching and Learning*

1 Introduction

When I came and visited it was all, I saw a lot of whites, I thought "whatever." Nothing new to me. You know, I never felt the prejudice. They ask me, "Don't you feel it?" or "Don't you see it?" And I say no, I don't. And I'm not out to look for it, either. To me that's trouble. And I'm not out to look for trouble. That'll bring me down, in my studies, as a person.

—Sylvia, a Latina basic writing student who had grown up in a multiethnic community

They looked at me crazy, you know. I guess they just knew I was from [an inner-city neighborhood] and I was supposed to have been in a gang or something. And they were afraid of me because of what I might do or they didn't trust me, with anything, like any of their possessions, or anything like that, there was a look on their face like that.

—Al, a basic writing student from a predominantly African-American inner-city neighborhood, describing his first days on campus

Before, when I just came to college, I was afraid that I wasn't going to survive. Because my English . . . they said you have to write just one paper . . . it was like if I was gonna die . . . because . . . I couldn't express myself, to start with. I was afraid.

—Christian, a basic writing student who had immigrated from El Salvador three years earlier

In Arizona I went to school with kids who were mostly all Indians, and there'd be, like, only four whites. And when I moved up here and went to school the first day I didn't know what to do. I wanted to go home, you know, I was so scared, I said, "I can't face these people." And I called my mom and told her, "I want to go home, this is not for me." But I stayed.

—Fannie, a basic writing student who had grown up on a Navajo reservation

3

Those of us who work with ethnically underrepresented and academically underprepared students are often visited by an itchy restlessness: a sense that we somehow are not taking optimal advantage of the opportunities before us, that we are not doing enough to prepare them for the unseen but inevitable rigors lurking just beyond our classroom doors. We sense a densely patterned diversity beneath the seamless labels that gather them into loose categories—*nonmainstream basic writers, linguistic and cultural minorities,* and so on—but we can only dimly intuit its many dimensions, let alone hope to meet all these varied instructional challenges. At times, we are moved to wonder at the audacity of institutional good intentions, at policies and programs that promise to cherish diversity and promote the academic success of these students—often in the absence of any fine-grained understanding of who they are, what their past and current struggles involve, and what sorts of support might help them. (Indeed, the very term *diversity* can so easily obscure a host of complexities, glossing over richly blended influences of culture, language, gender, and socioeconomic status.) Ironically, we come to realize that the rhetoric of policies and programs can become a sort of shield, a veil which obscures the many ways in which our efforts are missing the mark—that if we are to begin closing the recalcitrant gap between good will and substantive action, we need to still such rhetoric, to take a long, perhaps disconcerting, look at the knotty complexities of what *is.*

Such was the intention that informed this study—an examination of a peer-teaching program targeting underprepared and ethnically diverse student writers newly enrolled at a predominantly Anglo university,[1] a place where many clues pointed to a stubborn mismatch between a new "educational equity" policy and enduring realities. Although the campus mission statement had recently been amended to reflect a commitment "to providing quality education to students who are from groups historically underrepresented in higher education" and to "meeting and addressing the needs of these students," faculty, staff, and students continued to mirror the overwhelmingly white, middle-class demographics of the surrounding community. Meanwhile, the more fervent advocates of the equity policy often gave voice to cynical musings. The Academic Vice-President, for instance, shook his head in baffled resignation as he recited the simple insistence that he had heard from faculty again and again: "I'm not a bigot, I'm not biased, I treat all my students the same."

If students from outside the cultural and linguistic mainstream are to be treated equitably, they must, paradoxically, be offered special support, special opportunities; they must, in the end, challenge ethnocentric biases at the level of classroom and campus alike, moving others toward change even as they are being changed. The "passport" metaphor—taken from novelist George Lamming's observation that "language [is] a kind of passport" (1970, 154)[2]—becomes useful only as we understand the labyrinthine quality of these students' passage through the academy. If we are to offer meaningful support, we must understand that like all language learning, these students' struggles with academic writing are enmeshed in cultural learning (Heath 1986), in a larger grappling that is at once personal and public. While the final products of this struggle might be reflected in test scores, grade reports, and retention figures, its vicissitudes are played out upon a more elusive territory: in its daily unfolding and, particularly, in students' ongoing attempts to make sense of an unfamiliar social dialectic. The job of all instructors, but perhaps especially those who help with writing, is not simply to provide useful background knowledge or skills, but to invite students into this dialectic—a dialectic both intellectual and, because of its social nature, charged with feeling (Brand 1987; Bruner 1985; McLeod 1987; Werner 1948).

Peer-teaching programs represented a key component in this particular campus's efforts to extend such invitations to its growing population of equity students. Those enrolled in basic writing courses, for instance, were required to meet for three supplemental hours each week in small groups led by upper-division English majors—adjuncts[3] defended with the well-worn, but potentially plausible, claims of "individualizing instruction" and providing opportunities for "collaborative learning." Drawn to the cost-effectiveness of such assistance, program administrators also hoped that as these culturally diverse basic writers struggled with the seemingly impersonal, elusive sorts of discourse peculiar to their new environment, the groups would provide opportunities to gauge the effects of each student's written work in the presence of a real, comparatively nonthreatening audience. If, as Mina Shaughnessy (1977, 7) memorably observed of all basic writers, such students regard writing as "a line that moves haltingly across the page, exposing as it goes all that the writer doesn't know," then perhaps peer teachers could become someone besides the anticipated "stranger reading with a lawyer's eyes, looking for flaws." Perhaps peer teachers could help these students discover that vital nexus of the linguistic and the social, moving them to regard academic writing assignments as opportunities to express and communicate, to make meanings.

While such rationales gesture vaguely toward what has been said in print about successful peer-teaching programs elsewhere (see, for instance, Bruffee 1978, 1984; Hawkins 1980, 1990; Maxwell 1990), given the paucity of formal research in this area, the question of how such results might be replicated remains largely unexplored. At this campus, where faculty and administrators waxed enthusiastic about educational equity but remained deeply concerned about underpreparation, the peer-teaching program remained suspended among larger patterns of tension. Even as these conflicts quietly undercut attempts to offer cohesive guidance to adjunct staff, many faculty and administrators regarded the group leaders as significant players in campuswide equity efforts—because writing proficiency represents an important academic gatekeeper, and because these peer teachers were said to possess exceptional access to students' struggles with the written word.

But if their role was potentially valuable, so too was it riddled with dilemma. Still college students themselves, these peer teachers juggled substantial instructional challenges while simultaneously feeling their way toward an appropriate social stance—a stance which most described as existing somewhere between informal friendliness and formal authority and which, like all things ideal, could be only approximated, never definitively located. Relatively inexperienced, many adjuncts were overwhelmed not only by the social ambiguities of their task, but also by the urgency and complexity of its linguistic dimension. On the other hand, the group leaders did indeed possess generous access to students' worlds, and were often privy to rich information about the students' backgrounds and dreams—about their fears, their ideals, their reasons for coming to college, and the roadblocks and challenges that they were confronting. These peer teachers were, in other words, in ideal positions to peel away deceptively homogeneous labels, to move toward an appreciation of the depth and variety of their students' struggles to write for the academy as well as to acquire a sense of social membership, of belonging there. In the end, what these group leaders stood to discover was both essential and daunting: that their task, like the university's new equity mission, was a maze of richly varied, largely uncharted complexities.

Just as writing students enter into dialectical relationships with classroom and campus communities, so too are writing programs engaged in reciprocal patterns of influence—shaped by institutional goals and policies, but also helping shape these larger constructs. To appreciate this dynamic, one must look from multiple points of view, at multiple layers of meaning. Accordingly, this book examines both the instructional program and institutional context—ultimately seeking to promote not specific reforms but, rather, a way of seeing, a mode of reflection that might support practitioners' efforts to come to terms with their own complexities, to evaluate their own programs, to chart their own new directions.

Linguistic Minorities and the Academy: A Sociocultural Perspective

When students from nonmainstream backgrounds experiment with academic discourse, they are doing more than trying on a linguistic disguise; they are experimenting as well with new identities, new ways of thinking and being (Bartholomae 1985; Bizzell 1986; Brodkey 1987a; Rose 1989; Walvoord and McCarthy 1991). Increasingly, theorists and researchers acknowledge that the linguistic challenges that these students face are intricately connected to a broad web of cognitive, social, and affective concerns (Hull and Rose 1989, 1990; Hull et al. 1991), that these students navigate not only among ways of using language but, indeed, among worlds (Committee on CCCC Language Statement 1974). In so doing, notes Harris (1989, 17), they negotiate among a "polyphony of voices": the voices of their linguistically and culturally different home communities, the typically impersonal voices of their textbooks and professors, and, increasingly, the voices of student instructors, alternately authoritative and informal. Only over time can these disparate voices be merged into productive multiplicity; only over time can these students begin to integrate new influences and understandings, to move beyond initial conflict and uncertainty toward revised, pluralistic definitions of self (Bakhtin 1981; Cintron 1991; Fischer 1986; Severino 1992; Wertsch 1991).

While some theorists and practitioners suggest that small-group instruction can help all students find more confident voices in the academic conversation (see Bruffee 1978, 1984), such claims must be considered in light of the special challenges confronting linguistic and cultural minorities. As Valdés (1989) points out, findings from studies conducted with Anglo students are often inappropriately generalized, obscuring the particularized complexities of nonmainstream students' linguistic negotiations. Further, such struggles must be seen as more than *strictly* linguistic—as woven, rather, into contextual dynamics which not only influence the form and style of students' writing, but which also invest it with significance beyond the limited grappling with word or phrase.

Working with these students on writing assignments often requires an understanding of a complex interplay of group tendencies and individual differences, as well as insight into the political dilemmas—rooted in both the academic enterprise and the society at large—which attend their linguistic negotiations.

As the relatively low achievement levels and high attrition rates among some of our fastest-growing ethnic groups are chronicled by study after study (e.g., Astin 1982; California State Department of Education 1982, 1985; Carter and Wilson 1991; Center for Education Statistics 1986; Kaufman and Dolman 1984; National Commission on Secondary Education for Hispanics 1984), theorists and researchers have countered the "cognitive-deficit" or "cultural deprivation" thinking of 1960s researchers (e.g., Bereiter and Engelmann 1966; Deutsch et al. 1967; Hess and Shipman 1965; Jensen 1969) with explanations that acknowledge this webbing of the linguistic, social, and academic. Sociolinguistic research, for example, has depicted some of the ways in which patterns of language use in speech communities outside of school can conflict with the patterns expected in the classroom, thereby producing patterns of discontinuity said to contribute to teachers' tendencies to cast students' differences as deficiencies (e.g., Hymes 1972, 1974; Mehan 1978, 1980, 1987; Philips 1972, 1982). Meanwhile, anthropologist John Ogbu (1974, 1978, 1979, 1982, 1985, 1987; Ogbu and Matute-Bianchi 1986) has proposed an alternate explanation emphasizing minority populations' differential perceptions of access to the labor market. Distinguishing between "caste" and "immigrant" groups, Ogbu maintains that Hispanics and African Americans are unlikely to view schooling as a pathway to gainful employment; further, he maintains, children from these groups often see academic success as aligned with the adoption of a "white frame of reference," and therefore they "prefer peer solidarity to schoolwork," a tendency said to increase as these "caste-like" students move through the educational system (1987, 332–33; see also Fordham and Ogbu 1986).

Erickson (1987) notes that while both the cultural-mismatch and differential-labor-market arguments present plausible explanations, Ogbu's rather deterministic perspective underestimates the role of educators in promoting a more productive classroom experience for members of "caste" minorities. The key, he maintains, is to avoid calling attention to difference in a negative way, to abandon "hegemonic" classroom practices, and to work to convert politically charged "borders" into neutralized "boundaries" (351). In terms of linguistic growth, nonmainstream students must be encouraged to perceive the adoption of English (or the mainstream variety thereof) as "additive" rather than "subtractive" (Cummins 1986; Lambert 1977), to acquire the metalinguistic ability to reflect in a dispassionate manner upon the differences between the languages of community and classroom (Heath 1983, 1986).

Many believe that such change can be accomplished in part by a decentralization of power and increasing reliance upon "collaborative learning," arguments often buttressed with reference to Vygotsky's concept of "zones of proximal development" (1978), to the metaphor of "scaffolding" (Applebee and Langer 1983, 1986; Bruner 1978), and to empirical evidence that some nonmainstream students feel more at home in learning environments emphasizing peer networking (e.g., Labov 1982; Philips 1972, 1982).

Although research on teacher-student conferences (e.g., Beach 1986; Freedman 1981, 1987, 1992; Freedman and Katz 1987; Sperling and Freedman 1987; Sperling 1990) and peer response groups (e.g., DiPardo and Freedman 1988; Freedman 1992; Gere and Abbott 1985; Gere and Stevens 1985; Nystrand 1986) has begun to suggest how the familiar Vygotskian rationale can be enacted in specific teaching-learning interactions, "collaborative learning" remains a rubric perched with precarious authority over a broad array of programs. Educators, argues Erickson (1989, 431), are currently in the grips of a "crush on collaboration" which must be tempered by critical consideration of why and how it might be appropriate in particular instances.

Research Questions

By examining the role of these "collaborative" interactions in fostering the academic writing of linguistic-minority students, the present study begins to address several significant gaps in the existing literature; further, by considering the larger contexts of these teaching-learning encounters, the study situates the rationales and day-to-day functioning of the program within the sociopolitical matrix in which they were embedded. Examining not only the small-group interactions but also the basic writing program and campus "educational equity" mission of which they were an integral part, this research is predicated upon a belief that specific interactions cannot be understood apart from the contexts that shape and

define them—contexts which are, as Cazden (1988, 198) points out, inevitably "nested."
The study was guided by the following research questions:

1. What is the nature of the larger social contexts in which the basic writing adjunct program is situated—that is, at the level of the campus, the community in which it is located, and the university system of which it is a part? What tensions and controversies characterize the campus's efforts to promote "educational equity"?

2. What is the nature of the more immediate social context in which the program is situated—that is, at the level of the English department, as perceived from the points of view of the writing program directors, adjunct component coordinators, and instructors? What kind of initial training and continuing support do these small-group leaders receive? What tensions and controversies characterize efforts to institute the adjunct program?

3. How do the small-group leaders envision the nature of their task? How do they perceive their roles, and how do they define the purpose of the adjunct program? What are their perspectives upon linguistic and cultural diversity? What tensions and conflicts characterize these perspectives, and how do these relate to campuswide or departmental tensions and conflicts?

4. What is the nature of the kinds of struggles these ethnically diverse students face as they attempt to adjust at once to the demands of academic life and to a nearly all-white social environment? What is the nature of the responses they receive from the small-group leaders? How do students characterize these struggles? How do the small-group leaders characterize them?

Organization of the Book

Following a discussion of the research setting, design, and methods in chapter 2, I turn in chapter 3 to the first two research questions, considering the many tensions which attended the campus's efforts to meet the needs of equity students and locating the basic writing adjunct program within these uncertainties and controversies. Addressing the third research question, chapter 4 takes a close look at the two focal group leaders, Kalie and Morgan, describing their perspectives on their work and charting patterns of apparent contrast and underlying similarity. In chapters 5 through 8, I address the fourth research question, examining four focal students' backgrounds, attempts to adjust to college life, struggles with writing, and perceptions of the small-group component of their basic writing course. Finally, chapter 9 reflects upon the complexities of designing effective programs to serve the needs of linguistically and culturally diverse basic writers, and discusses the more general ramifications of one campus's often troubled attempts to provide equitable opportunities for all.

Endnotes

1. Acknowledging that groups traditionally termed *minorities* would soon comprise a majority of this particular state's population, systemwide administrators preferred the label *equity students;* I use that designation as well as the terms *nonmainstream, ethnic-minority, linguistic-minority,* and *cultural-minority students.* Lacking more accurately descriptive and politically neutral terms, I use *Anglo* and *white* interchangeably to designate non-Hispanic whites.

2. A longer passage from Lamming's book appears on page 91.

3. Members of the campus community called the small-group component of the basic writing course a *tutorial* program and its staff members *tutors.* In order to avoid misleading associations with writing centers and one-on-one assistance, I am using different terms throughout this study—*writing adjunct* or *peer teaching* to describe the program as a whole, and *small-group leaders, peer teachers,* or *adjuncts* to describe the program's staff.

2 The Study: Setting, Design, and Procedures

This study's objectives—to consider particular instructional interactions from multiple points of view, and to locate these interactions within layers of institutional context—strongly suggested an ethnographic approach (Erickson, Florio, and Buschman 1980; Bogdan and Biklen 1982; Erickson 1986). As detailed in the following discussion, the research site and subjects were selected in the interests of developing a finely textured, richly contextualized portrait of efforts to meet the needs of nonmainstream students. Data consisted primarily of informants' own words (in interviews, small-group sessions, and informal encounters).

The Research Setting

The Community and Campus

The campus in question—to be called, pseudonymously, Dover Park University (DPU)—was located in Dover Park, a suburban, middle-class community in which whites comprised, as of 1990, an 85 percent majority. While it was a prosperous town, with a total population which increased from 23,000 to almost 35,000 between 1980 and 1990, its non-Anglo population had been growing at a comparative snail's pace. Located in a western state in which whites were fast becoming a minority, a scant one-hour's drive from an urban area of marked diversity, Dover Park remained a place where almost everyone was Anglo and middle class. A carefully planned community of tract housing developments, neighborhood parks, and modest shopping centers, it looked tidy but uninspired, prosperous but not affluent. The university was attractive but unimposing, its angular concrete buildings softened in recent years by handsome landscaping, its native flatness modified by grassy berms.

Although part of a bustling system of state-financed colleges and surrounded by burgeoning suburbs, only recently had DPU begun to boost its sagging enrollments and overcome a longstanding reputation for mediocrity. A prickly period of faculty-administration discord had ended in the early 1980s with the resignation of DPU's controversial President, and in the mid 1980s the campus and community welcomed the down-to-earth, confident leadership of his permanent replacement. Described in the local press as "a mild-mannered, warm-handshake kind of fellow who looks like your favorite uncle," the new President's quiet competence calmed battle-worn faculty and strengthened community-campus relations. "Even in the days of its worst reputation," he maintained in a recent newspaper article, "this was never a poor institution." His leadership helped convince once-reluctant locals that the campus was a respectable option after all, and they were soon enrolling in record numbers.

From the fall of 1985 to the fall of 1989, DPU's total enrollment increased from around 5,500 to around 7,000, imparting a new air of prosperity, but also straining available resources. While students of color remained a small minority, their numbers were also increasing: during these same years, total African-American enrollment rose from 172 to 245, Mexican-American enrollment from 124 to 215, and Native American enrollment from 49 to 75. Even in the fall of 1989, however, the campus remained 77 percent Anglo, and officials worried about the large numbers of ethnic-minority students who were leaving the campus without graduating. Faced with a rapid rise in overall enrollment and growing pressure to increase minority representation, administrators struggled to balance commitment to the equity mission against efforts to expand existing programs and services.

Dover Park University was chosen as a research site not because its process of transition seemed in any way exceptional or exemplary. It was, rather, an ordinary campus not unlike countless others around the country—ostensibly prosperous but increasingly stretched thin, its administrators and faculty well-intentioned but sometimes weighed down by entrenched attitudes and precedents. By turns blessed and cursed with a modest array of strengths and weaknesses, triumphs and perplexities, DPU faced the task of becoming a multicultural campus with uneven, unremarkable resources. In this sense, it seemed a promising place to explore the problematic role of college writing programs in accommodating linguistic and cultural diversity, to unpackage some of the densely woven complexity that so often resides within the commonplace.

Promoting Educational Equity: An Array of Programs

By the spring of 1990, campus officials had begun to struggle in earnest with the many issues attending DPU's newly announced commitment to educational equity. Although some insisted that dilemmas yet outnumbered solutions, to ask any administrator what efforts were being made to ensure the academic and social success of ethnically diverse students was to call forth a litany of programs and services. While peer teaching was often mentioned as a noteworthy addition, it tended to be dwarfed by this lengthening list of other activities, each with its own acronym, funding sources, qualifying criteria, purposes, and reporting relationships. Some were well-known national programs, others organizations peculiar to this university system or campus. When considered together, they seem at first glance more crazy-quilt than ordered patchwork:

- *Educational Support Services (ESS)* included the state-funded Educational Opportunity Program (EOP), the oldest student-equity program on this and most other campuses, providing academic advising and financial support to low-income students. While at many campuses over 90 percent of EOP students are from non-Anglo backgrounds, at DPU this was typically true of approximately two-thirds. Other ESS projects included the federally funded Summer Bridge program, designed to promote pre-freshman-year readiness, primarily for underrepresented ethnic students; federally funded Learning Skills Services, which provided academic assistance in general education coursework to low-income students; and state- and lottery-funded Pre-College programs, designed to promote early recruitment of ethnic minority students.

- *The Comprehensive Learning Project (CLP)* provided first-year academic assistance and developmental coursework to students scoring in the bottom quartile on math and/or writing placement tests. While along with EOP it was often referred to as a key equity program at DPU, ethnicity was not a criterion for inclusion in either program. Indeed, since the program's inception, over half the students designated CLP had been white; of the 218 first-time freshmen designated CLP during the fall semester of 1989, for instance, 136 indicated "non-Hispanic White" on an ethnicity questionnaire.

• *The Inter-Cultural Center* was staffed by EOP but housed in the Student Union. Its director helped guide and coordinate the activities of four ethnic-student clubs: M.E.Ch.A. (Movimiento Estudiantil Chicano de Aztlan), Black Student Union, Asian Pacific Islanders Association, and Native American Student Alliance. Intended to provide outlets for expression of cultural history and experience, these organizations sponsored a number of campus events: celebrations, educational forums, and other cultural awareness activities.

• *The Faculty-Student Mentoring Program* was designed to provide enrichment activities and academic guidance to ethnically diverse students. The program's title was something of a misnomer, since faculty mentors were increasingly supported by upper-division students—an evolution that moved one administrator to refer to it as a "glorified peer advising program." Despite such criticisms and an ongoing paucity of ethnic mentors, many administrators regarded the program as particularly promising. It was funded by the state lottery.

• *Tutorial Services* were offered through a number of sources, including the CLP, ESS-sponsored Learning Skills Services, an Associated Students-funded Tutorial Center, and various academic departments. Though these programs served varying concentrations of ethnic minority students, all were commonly named as de facto equity support services.

Not surprisingly, many noted the difficulty of coordinating all these disparate avenues of student support, their diverse funding sources and reporting relationships sometimes compartmentalizing what were in fact overlapping functions. In an effort to set up dialogue among these many factions and to involve faculty in meeting the needs of ethnically diverse students, the Vice-President for Academic Affairs had recently created the Educational Equity Advisory Council, chaired by the Dean of Students and including members from administrative as well as academic units across the campus. This body received reports from three subcommittees, each of which was chaired by an academic dean: the Educational Equity Subcommittee on Faculty Involvement, the Educational Equity Subcommittee on Outreach and Retention, and the Educational Equity Subcommittee on Campus Climate. Students, faculty, and administrators sat together on each of these subcommittees—evaluating programs, highlighting problems, brainstorming solutions, and formulating educational objectives which sought to involve the campus as a whole. Included among a set of such goals that the committees had submitted to DPU's President were a number of pragmatic concerns ("To establish a comprehensive skills development program, and avoid conflict and overlap among present entities charged with these duties") as well as statements of lofty ideals ("To enhance positive interactions between underrepresented cultures and the campus at large in order to create a climate in which diversity is not merely tolerated but is cherished").

The Basic Writing Program

As the campus struggled to translate "educational equity" slogans into practice, faculty and administrators agreed that the basic writing program represented an important link in efforts to retain students of color, many of whom were receiving strikingly low scores on the statewide writing placement exam. It was, like all DPU's equity efforts, a link not easily forged: if the basic writing program reflected the complexities of DPU's response to diversity, so too did these "basic writers" reflect the complexities of ethnic students' responses to DPU. Even in the brief overview which follows, one begins to sense not only the good intentions behind the program but also the web of political issues in which it was situated.

Overview of the Basic Writing Curriculum: History and Present Organization

DPU's English department first acknowledged the need for basic writing instruction back in the late 1970s, when it became clear that a growing number of students were finding freshman composition an insurmountable challenge. Initially reluctant to institute a basic writing course, the department developed a tutorial program which provided one to three hours of individualized instruction to students needing supplemental help with class assignments. Although the tutoring staff was given only a few hours' training and was rather informally supervised by the course instructors and freshman composition director, longtime members of the English department recalled the generally positive response that the program had received early on. Any misgivings attending the program focused on underpreparation rather than educational equity, since most of the students receiving tutoring were, like nearly everyone else on campus at the time, white and middle-class.

Holding that "remedial" coursework did not belong at a four-year institution, some faculty insisted that the tutorial program was as far as the campus should go in providing extra help with writing. Then, as increasing numbers of culturally and linguistically diverse students joined the ranks of those needing such help—and as pressure mounted to promote such students' progress toward graduation—the need for a basic writing course became compellingly clear. The first section of English 90, "The Basic Writing Workshop," met in the spring of 1983, and more sections were added each semester in the ensuing years. In contrast to campuswide demographics, these classes invariably enrolled large numbers of non-Anglo students—a preponderance of African Americans and Mexican Americans from urban centers elsewhere in the state and a scattering of recent immigrants from other countries.

Initially, the English department held firm that any student failing the basic writing course twice should be academically disqualified. Over time, however, as the campus realized that those failing the course one or more times included a number of students from underrepresented ethnic groups, support grew for a two-semester course sequence that might better address the needs of students receiving especially low scores on the placement exam. Reluctant to involve itself in yet another tier of "remedial coursework," the English department was united in the belief that students requiring more rudimentary help should enroll instead at the local junior college. Although such a lower-level basic writing course was indeed added to the campus curriculum in the mid 1980s, it was placed under the auspices of the newly instituted Comprehensive Learning Project (CLP), and only loosely linked to the English department's share of the basic writing curriculum.

With the inception of the Comprehensive Learning Project, incoming freshmen receiving bottom-quartile placement exam scores were required to pass first-semester "Writing Skills" and "Reading Skills" courses, this before going on to English 90, which became for these students the second half of a full year's basic writing instruction. (As before, those with scores deemed only slightly subpar were required to pass only English 90 before going on to freshman composition.) To enhance articulation between the first- and second-semester basic writing courses, a plan was devised whereby some English 90 sections were set aside for CLP students; that is, while staffed and supervised by the English department, these sections enrolled only students who had been required to complete the CLP basic writing course.

Both the English department and the Comprehensive Learning Project supported a system of adjunct assistance for students enrolled in basic writing courses. (By the late 1980s, both had largely abandoned efforts to provide one-on-one tutoring in favor of small discussion groups.) Although the English department's and CLP's basic writing programs remained entirely separate in terms of funding and supervision, interprogram communication was enhanced by the fact that a number of instructors taught both the CLP first-semester course and English 90; virtually all were part-time, non-tenure-track employees (as was the CLP Director), and a movement was gradually gathering momentum in the English department to turn over its basic writing courses to graduate-student instructors.[1] By a mandate from statewide headquarters, course sections were kept to a maximum of fifteen students in both programs.

Because it was older, larger, and supervised by tenured professors who were also composition specialists, the English department's adjunct program seemed more likely to represent the campus's response to underprepared equity students. This program, described in the following subsection, was therefore selected as the focus of the present study.

The English 90 Adjunct Program

Individualized tutoring was first replaced by more cost-effective group assistance in the fall of 1985, and by the time data were collected in the spring of 1990, the small-group adjunct program had come to be regarded as well established. Although all basic writing students were required to attend the small groups for three hours each week (typically just before or after the regular class), given the economy of the arrangement, the fifteen or so group leaders employed by the program during data collection provided more than enough coverage.

The adjunct staff was hired and supervised by the freshman composition director, who required prospective group leaders to fill out an application form requesting the names of faculty references, background information such as major and class level, and a narrative account of relevant "academic and work experience." As had reportedly been the case throughout the history of the program, during the spring of 1990 all staff members were English majors. The only fully bilingual group leader, a young Taiwanese woman, worked primarily with immigrant students. The staff also included a young woman said by the freshman composition director to be the first African American ever employed by the program. All the others were Anglo and, to my knowledge, monolinguals.

Although small-group leaders were not required to complete a formal training program, they were invited to attend the two or three adjunct staff meetings held each semester, which provided opportunities to share experiences and receive advice from the freshman composition director and other group leaders. They were also urged to take the English department's course in theoretic and practical issues in the teaching of composition, and some reported that coursework through the education department had also proven helpful.

In order to assist the freshman composition director with the administrative details of running the basic writing adjunct program, in the fall of 1987 the position of student assistant/"adjunct coordinator" had been created. Before the start of each fall semester, a senior-year member of the adjunct staff was selected to serve in that capacity for the coming academic year. (During the spring of 1990, this individual was paid $8 an hour, a slightly higher wage than the $6.85–$7.10 allotted the other staff members.) The adjunct coordinator helped assign group leaders to course sections, collected vouchers, distributed paychecks, attended all staff meetings, and sometimes lent a listening ear to group leaders needing to talk through problems or issues.

At the start of each semester the adjunct coordinator assigned three group leaders to work with each English 90 section; the course instructors then assigned each of the three to a group of five students, with whom they typically worked for the duration of the semester. Instructors varied considerably in terms of the amount of time spent guiding the work of group leaders—some taking a "hands-off" approach, some planning their work in substantial detail, most falling somewhere between these extremes.

Research Participants

Campus Administrators

In order to answer my first research question concerning the nature of the campus as a whole, I interviewed administrators responsible for designing and implementing the campus equity policy. Since DPU's educational equity efforts tended to be diffuse and loosely coordinated, my list of relevant campus individuals continued to grow and change as I explored the campus, conducted initial interviews, and heard mention of the roles being played by an array of administrative offices. In the end, I interviewed a total of seven administrators at the campus level: the Directors of the CLP and EOP, who were frequently named as "key equity administrators"; the Dean of Academic Programs, who oversaw the CLP; the Dean of Students, who oversaw the EOP and the campus Inter-Cultural Center and who also chaired an influential Educational Equity subcommittee on student recruitment; the Associate Dean for Student Life, who helped coordinate an assortment of student organizations; a campus dean who chaired an Educational Equity subcommittee on student retention and who would soon become Acting Academic Vice-President[2]; and the Coordinator of the campuswide, interdisciplinary Tutorial Services funded by the Associated Students.

Writing Program Administrators and Staff

In order to explore the more immediate context of the program—that is, the English department which was responsible for the program's design and administration—I also interviewed a number of individuals within the writing program. Two of these (the freshman and upper-division composition directors) were respected senior members of the department who had shared the responsibility of running the writing program for over twenty years; another was a slightly younger professor who had recently completed a brief and controversial stint as writing program director. I also interviewed the present adjunct coordinator, his immediate predecessor, and the four instructors currently teaching the English department's basic writing course.

The Course Instructor

Since the small groups were attached to various sections of the Basic Writing Workshop, I also wished to locate these peer-teaching interactions within the context of the faculty-taught course. In selecting a section on which to focus, I was particularly interested in finding an instructor who was deemed both effective and fairly representative of the program as a whole. Susan Williams (like all proper names used herein, this is a pseudonym), whose course I ultimately chose, fit both criteria rather nicely. A former full-time community college instructor who had taught basic writing at DPU for several years, Williams was highly regarded by colleagues in the Comprehensive Learning Project, where she served as "lead" writing instructor, and in the English department, where she taught composition and literature courses. As the CLP's lead writing instructor, she was responsible for guiding curricula, giving inservice workshops attended by other CLP instructors, serving on staffing committees, and helping build bridges between the CLP's and English department's basic writing programs. Impressed by her insight and forthright, efficient manner, the Dean of Academic Programs appointed her Acting CLP Director for a two-month period during the spring of 1990; and when the regular Director resigned shortly after the conclusion of data collection, Williams assumed that position on a permanent basis.[3] She was, in other words, deeply immersed in the instructional challenges that I wished to consider, but she was also in a particularly good position to observe how the CLP's work was situated within the larger contexts of the writing program and campus equity mission. In a program in which all the instructors were part-time, non-tenure-track employees, Williams was in some ways a typical staff member, but also an unusually well regarded and influential one.

The Group Leaders

Although the decision of which group leaders to assign to Susan Williams's section was ultimately up to the composition director, he graciously allowed me to screen potential candidates. I asked for recommendations from the composition director, Williams, and the adjunct coordinator, emphasizing that I was again looking for staff members deemed particularly effective in their work, believing that these "best-case scenarios" would provide the clearest lens for observing the dynamics of the program. As several recommended individuals reported that they would be unavailable in the spring, I eventually narrowed my list to three—Lenora, Kalie, and Morgan—all of whom were then assigned by the composition director to the section that I wished to study. (Since the adjunct staff was predominantly female, gender balance did not seem particularly important.)

In the first weeks of the semester, I tape-recorded, observed, and chatted with all three group leaders, and by the third week had selected Kalie and Morgan as the focal leaders. Both were upper-division English majors in their late twenties who were widely regarded as effective group leaders, successful students, and high-profile presences on campus. During February of 1990, for instance, each received a prestigious and well-publicized campus award: Kalie won a DPU essay contest, the prize for which was a summer's residency at a Bulgarian university, while Morgan was awarded a "predoctoral" fellowship, which funded her attendance at the 1990 annual convention of the Conference on College Composition and Communication (CCCC) and at a summer workshop for underrepresented students considering doctoral study.

Since I was interested in observing patterns of variation, I was particularly drawn to the fact that Kalie and Morgan also presented a number of striking contrasts in terms of background, aspirations, and approaches to working with students. For instance, Kalie often played the part of mentor to new staff members, and offered frequent reminders that she was arguably the most experienced group leader on campus, having worked in the adjunct program for over three years; Morgan, on the other hand, had joined the program only the semester before, and had never worked with CLP students. Kalie assumed a directive, talkative stance in her interactions with students; Morgan, having attended a number of workshops on collaborative learning, was trying hard to assume an increasingly lower profile. Kalie was a playful and enthusiastic writer, Morgan a dutiful and sometimes struggling one; Kalie saw her work with students as a way to earn money, while Morgan, who planned to become a teacher, saw it as a testing ground for strategies that she might later employ in her high school classroom. Finally, Kalie was, like nearly everyone who had ever been employed by the program, Anglo; Morgan was DPU's first-ever African-American peer teacher, although having grown up in the predominantly white county in which DPU is located, she did not speak Black English and had no close African-American friends. As a member of the Anglo middle class, Kalie seemed keenly aware that equity students came from worlds quite different from her own; Morgan, on the other hand, negotiated a far more ambiguous territory, sometimes communicating feisty solidarity with equity students, at other times acutely aware of the boundaries of class and culture which set her apart.

The Focal Students

Like the group leaders, the four focal students were selected because they were maximally contrasting—balanced in terms of gender and personality (two were female, two male; two were reserved, two outgoing) and presenting a rich array of linguistic backgrounds and orientations to writing. Two were from Kalie's group: Al, a reserved African American who tried to conceal the fact that he had grown up speaking Black English, and the gregarious Christian, who had immigrated from El Salvador three years earlier and was still struggling with the demands of both spoken and written English. The other two were from Morgan's group: Fannie, a bashful Native American who had grown up on a Navajo reservation, and Sylvia, an outgoing Latina who had been born in Mexico but raised in an integrated, multiethnic community in the United States. Although all four students were loosely grouped under the same campus labels—all, for instance, had been designated both EOP and CLP—each found particular challenges in the act of composing and in the larger process of adjusting to life at this predominantly Anglo campus. All four attended both the lecture and small-group sessions with reasonable regularity and handed in most class assignments. Thus, while I had also selected three backups, I was able to follow these four first-choice focal students throughout the semester.

Overview of Data Collection Procedures

Summarized in table 1, data sources were both numerous and varied—this in the interests of compiling a fine-grained picture composed of various individuals' points of view, and to help correct any biases that I brought to my initial observations (Erickson 1986; Goetz and LeCompte 1984). Over the spring 1990 semester, data were collected concurrently at the campus level and within the various layers of the writing program; indeed, the one came to inform the other, since my list of campus-level informants grew and changed as I observed small-group leaders and students, conducted initial interviews, and began to understand the larger contexts of the adjunct program.

Campus Data Collection

In answering my first research question, which addressed the nature of the campus as a whole, I relied primarily upon tape-recorded interviews with campus administrators as a primary data source. While these interviews consistently probed the role of administrators' various offices in the campus equity mission, prompts were tailored to fit their widely divergent backgrounds and current responsibilities. These interviews were fairly open-ended and conversational: often, administrators would talk in fluent detail in response to rather general prompts (e.g., "Tell me about your

Table 1

Data Collection Record

Source	Number
At the campus level	
• Tape-recorded interviews with administrators who played various roles in promoting "educational equity" on the campus (the Director of a campuswide tutorial program, EOP Director, CLP Director, Dean of Academic Programs, Dean of Students, Associate Dean for Student Life, and Academic Vice-President)	7
• Audiotapes of campus events relating to cultural diversity (e.g., lectures, addresses, and workshops)	4
• Newspaper articles relating to campus equity issues	30
At the level of the English department	
• Tape-recorded interviews with the present composition director, two past composition directors, four basic writing instructors, the present adjunct coordinator, and a past adjunct coordinator	9
At the level of the adjunct program	
• Beginning- and end-of-term interviews with the classroom teacher, two focal group leaders, and four focal students	14
• Audiotapes of the focal students' regular basic writing class (all class sessions for the first three weeks of the semester, then one session per week for the duration)	24
• Audiotapes of all the focal adjuncts' small-group sessions (three hours per week for the entire semester)	66
• Semester-long teaching journals (in which adjuncts reflected upon their work, particularly with focal students)	2
• Audiotapes of adjunct staff meetings (an administrative meeting at the beginning of the semester, two trouble-shooting sessions during the first weeks of the semester, and Susan Williams's meeting with the focal adjuncts)	4
• Photocopies of all drafts of each assignment for each of the focal students	57
• Focal students' journals (compendiums of freewrites and informal class assignments)	4
• Placement exam scores for each focal student	4
• Background questionnaires completed by each focal student	4
• Instructor's final evaluations on each focal student	4
Other data sources	
• Statistical information regarding campus demographics and programs (obtained from the Dean of Administrative Services)	
• Fieldnotes (covering course lectures, adjunct staff meetings, and informal encounters with various participants)	
• Fieldwork journal (a more subjective, reflective account of my observations)	

program's involvement with the campus equity mission"), and would elaborate freely as I probed and followed up. These interviews generally lasted around one hour, and covered varied territory: for instance, the Academic Vice-President spoke at length about his perceptions of the many tensions running through the campus's response to minority students; the Dean of Academic Programs detailed lingering faculty misgivings about the academic consequences of the new equity policy; the Dean of Students and Associate Dean for Student Life described the role of student support services and organizations; the Directors of the CLP and EOP reflected upon their efforts to meet the needs of underprepared equity students; and the Coordinator of the Associated Students Tutorial Services shared her perspectives on the role of peer teaching in the university.

As the link between the adjunct program and broader efforts to promote ethnic diversity at DPU became increasingly clear, additional sources of data were gathered which allowed further exploration of these relationships. These included newspaper articles describing local controversies of concern to two of the focal students, and audiotapes of various events which signaled campus officials' growing interest in promoting an understanding of cultural diversity. As one of the focal students became deeply involved in pledging an African-American fraternity, additional background materials were gathered on the history and significance of African-American Greek organizations. Finally, statistical data were obtained from the Dean of Administrative Services which allowed me to locate the focal students within the overall demographics of the campus.

English Department Data Collection

In order to answer my second research question, I conducted interviews with nine individuals within the English department who had played various key roles in designing and implementing the basic writing program. For instance, a former director of freshman composition was asked about the rationale for instituting a basic writing course, the conflict which attended its inception, and the evolution of the adjunct program; a controversial professor who briefly served as freshman composition director was asked for his views on the adjunct program and what he had hoped to accomplish in it; and the current director of freshman composition, whose duties included directing the basic writing adjunct program (i.e., hiring and supervising staff), was asked for his perspectives on the program's purpose and on the needs of the students it served. In addition to the instructor whose class and small-group component were followed for this project, three of the department's other basic writing instructors were interviewed regarding their thoughts on the adjunct program and attempts to integrate the work of group leaders into their course sections. Finally, past and present adjunct coordinators were asked about their administrative support roles and, more generally, about their thoughts on the program's function and usefulness. Like the interviews described above, these were semi-standardized conversations. (A listing of all interview questions appears in the appendix.)

Program Data Collection

To answer the remaining research questions concerning the nature of the small-group sessions and the students' responses, I pulled information from varied data sources, which allowed a fine-grained look at the role of the adjunct program in addressing students' needs.

I attended and tape-recorded all adjunct staff meetings over the semester of data collection. These meetings were relatively infrequent: one was scheduled in January for strictly administrative purposes (completing needed paperwork, etc.), and two additional one-hour discussion meetings were held early in the term (these were primarily troubleshooting sessions, providing opportunities for the group leaders to share concerns and receive advice from one another as well as from the freshman composition director).

In order to situate the small-group sessions within the regular class, throughout the first month of the semester I attended each class, taping the session and taking fieldnotes; for the remainder of the semester, I attended at least once a week, usually on the day that a new writing assignment was given. During these sessions, the instructor's expectations for the various assignments were made explicit, thereby framing the later work of small-group leaders and students on each essay. My attendance at the regular class also provided opportunities to observe the interface between the two events; often, for instance, students would continue to talk in class about issues discussed during the adjunct hour, or, conversely, students would ask group leaders to clarify something that the instructor had said at the previous whole-class meeting. Although most of the group leaders' and the instructor's attempts to coordinate their efforts took the form of brief, impromptu conversations in the hall (these were recorded, when I happened to witness them, in my fieldnotes), they did hold a single one-hour meeting in March; I also attended this meeting, taping and taking notes.

I tape-recorded and observed both small-group leaders' thrice-weekly sessions over the entire semester of data collection. In order that I might be as unobtrusive as possible, I dropped off audiotape recorders at the beginning of each session and situated myself in a corner of the room where I could visually observe group interactions and note students' comings and goings. Although I advised the small-group participants that they could turn off the tape recorders anytime they felt uncomfortable, they did so only on rare occasions.

I also collected beginning- and end-of-term interviews with the small-group leaders, focal students, and classroom teacher. (See the appendix for interview protocols.) For the most part, these interviews followed what has been called a "guide" (Patton 1990) or "semi-standardized" approach (Merriam 1988); that is, although the wording of most questions was formulated in advance to ensure coverage of the same general themes across the various interviews, many responses were followed up with impromptu probes, and interviewees were allowed to wander from the prescribed agenda. While the interviews were standardized to an extent, the format allowed for considerable flexibility and conversational give-and-take. All interviewees were asked for their perceptions of the efficacy of the adjunct program and, more broadly, their perceptions of the challenges before ethnic minority students at this predominantly white institution. The small-group leaders and teacher were asked about their philosophies of instruction, their understandings of the instructional needs of the focal students, and their efforts to meet these needs; students were asked about their own perceptions of their needs and of the effectiveness of the class and adjunct component. In end-of-term interviews with focal students and small-group leaders, segments of small-group audiotapes were played back, and interpretations and responses were solicited. These segments were selected for stimulated recall because they indicated pivotal moments or highlighted issues or themes that ran consistently through the small-group leaders' and students' work over the semester (on the uses of stimulated recall in composition research, see DiPardo, in press; Rose 1984).

A number of additional data sources supplemented these small-group and interview audiotapes. Throughout the semester, factual records of meetings, informal encounters with various research participants, whole-class sessions, and so forth were recorded in fieldwork notes. I also kept a fieldwork journal, defined by Spradley (1980, 71) as a more subjective record of "experiences, ideas, fears, mistakes, confusions, breakthroughs, and problems." Besides providing an outlet for reflecting upon unresolved questions and dilemmas arising over the course of data collection, the journal became a record of my personal biases and responses, and was also helpful in documenting my effects (see "Researcher's Role," below). I additionally asked the two focal group leaders to reflect upon their work in regular journals; both agreed, and their journals became an additional data source.

Because the course instructor collected each student's work in a cumulative portfolio over the semester, I was able to borrow the focal students' folders periodically and make photocopies of all class assignments to date; this included ongoing student journals, various homework assignments, and rough drafts and revisions of each regular writing assignment (the latter containing the instructor's comments, suggestions, and grades).[4] I also photocopied from focal student portfolios a beginning-of-term background questionnaire as well as the instructor's end-of-term written assessments and recommendations. Focal students' initial writing placement test scores from the fall of 1989 were obtained from the Comprehensive Learning Project office.

Data Analysis

I reviewed each interview tape within a week, compiling complete transcriptions interspersed with italicized notations of my responses and interpretations. Group tapes were normally reviewed the same day on which they were collected, my notes consisting of a summary of visual observations and group attendance, detailed accounts of each group's discussion, italicized notations of my responses and interpretations, and, often, transcriptions of passages that seemed particularly pertinent to my research questions.

Over time, I combed repeatedly through the total data set to identify themes and patterns of tension that had repeatedly emerged as salient (Bogdan and Biklen 1982; Spradley 1980). As I sifted through my interviews with campus administrators, for instance, I identified two prevalent tensions (i.e., strong support for the equity policy tempered by worries about ethnic separatism and academic standards); once I had identified this pattern, I went back over the interview transcripts to collect all relevant statements, and then selected several that seemed particularly representative. To be sure of the stability of the pattern, I made repeated passes through the total data set to look for any disconfirming evidence or counterexamples. I went through a similar process in analyzing data at the levels of the writing program and adjunct program, identifying five tensions which ran through the statements of staff at both levels. Finally, I combed through my data on the four focal students, identifying information about their cultural and linguistic backgrounds, their struggles with writing, their group leaders' responses, and the students' own perspectives on the small-group sessions.

In the end, I was able to pull from multiple data sources to discuss each issue or theme, supporting all conclusions with detailed reference to the perspectives of various informants, to particular instructional interactions, to student writing, or to background statistical data. Although these interpretations are well supported for this particular setting, their external validity ultimately rests upon the readers' ability to "generalize personally to their own situations" (McCutcheon 1981)—to locate comparable patterns of reflection upon their own contexts, and to discover fresh directions of inquiry and discussion (Merriam 1988; Walker 1980).

Researcher's Role

Gaining Entry and Assessing My Effects

My relationship with Dover Park University and its basic writing program began long before the inception of this research. I was a part-time composition instructor at DPU a number of years ago, and taught some of the first basic writing courses the campus offered. The current and past composition directors were former colleagues who knew me quite well, and most of the campus administrators interviewed for this study were at least passing acquaintances from my period of employment.

To course instructor Susan Williams and virtually all the group leaders, on the other hand, I was at the outset a complete stranger. Hoping to overcome my outsider status, I provided each with a written description of my proposed project, invited them to ask questions about what I was doing, and chatted with them informally about my interest in their work. By the end of the first month of data collection, I had the sense that all were quite comfortable; and while Williams noted that she thought they might all be trying a little harder than usual, she and the group leaders reported that they did not find the tape recorders distracting.

My decision to absent myself from the small-group sessions (relying upon audiotapes, distanced visual observation, and supplementary conversations with group leaders and students) reflected my desire to be as unobtrusive as possible. A number of group leaders and students had suggested that my presence during these sessions would make them self-conscious; I did find, however, that I was able to take advantage of many opportunities to chat informally with adjunct staff and students before and after both the lecture and small-group segments, which were separated by a fortuitous ten-minute break. Further, as noted above, I stayed in the vicinity of the group sessions throughout each hour, periodically observing from a distance and, on rare occasions, working individually with students when their group leaders were absent or otherwise engaged.

As Kalie and Morgan became more comfortable with me, both would occasionally reflect in my presence upon their interactions with particular students. Seldom would they ask me directly what I had learned about the four focal students, but their curiosity about my conversations with students was often apparent. Kalie and particularly Morgan often seemed hungry for professional conversation, sometimes just needing to muse aloud in the presence of an interested onlooker. While I encouraged them to talk with me, I refrained from volunteering information about particular students, emphasizing instead my more general sense of the complexities of their work (all such conversations were recorded in my fieldwork journal). When pressed for my insights into particular students, I would often respond by noting how rich and interesting an individual was, and by urging the leaders to ask the student about his or her background.

As Morgan made plans to attend the 1990 CCCC annual convention in Chicago, she expressed an interest in traveling together; as it turned out, we sat in adjacent seats on both flights, and also shared a hotel room during our stay. During those several days, we engaged in countless conversations, not only about conference events, but also about Morgan's many personal and professional quandaries. While I stuck to my resolve to deflect questions about particular students, I found myself revealing more of my own educational philosophies than at any time previously. Although I wondered initially if these conversations would alter the course of Morgan's work to any extent, as I continued my observations and quizzed Morgan about what she had taken away from the convention, I came to realize that our conversations had been of little consequence.

(As detailed in chapter 4, several convention workshops on collaborative learning did, however, have a marked impact.)

Though Morgan shared my penchant for mulling over complexities to a greater extent than Kalie, both preferred knowledge of specific strategies to brooding reflection over many-layered meanings. While they were interested in talking with me about their work and, sometimes, in gathering my perceptions, they did not at all see me as an "expert" or someone whom they had to work extra hard to impress. I suspect that while my constant questions probably encouraged the group leaders to reflect a bit more upon the complexities of their work than they would otherwise, both noted that they were relatively unaffected by their participation in my study. Over time, whatever performance anxiety that they may have felt initially seemed to disappear more or less completely; while I no doubt had some impact upon their thinking and approaches, my effects appeared to be small indeed.

Although my relations with the two group leaders were affable, the many differences between us (e.g., in age, personality, and background) tended to promote a certain distance. This was less the case with the course instructor, Susan Williams, whom I began to count as a friend. Though often pressed for time, she always seemed to enjoy the opportunity to talk about what was on her mind (these conversations were also recorded regularly in my fieldwork journal). While the fact that I provided an ongoing sounding board may have exerted a subtle influence, since Williams was so much the confident veteran and practiced analyst of her own work, I suspect my presence was welcome but not particularly influential.

Therefore, in terms of Spradley's (1980, 58) taxonomy, mine could be called a "moderate" level of participation, balanced among my history as "insider" on the one hand (i.e., someone who formerly taught in this program and who knew many of the faculty members and administrators), my initial status as a relative stranger to the group leaders and teacher, and my gradual transformation into a trusted, slightly more participatory observer.

Researcher Bias

Observing that all efforts to relate experience are infused with ideology, Linda Brodkey (1987b, 48) argues that remaining silent is hardly a tenable alternative to the "scholarly vulnerability" of ethnographic approaches.

While I have tried as much as possible to let my informants speak for themselves, this account is of course informed by such vulnerability, constructed by a human being with cultural and political biases—by a person struggling, to use a term that emerged as key in my analysis and this report, with inner "tensions" of her own.

A middle-class Anglo, I have lived and worked most of my adult life in communities not unlike Dover Park, and much of what I heard from staff members during my months of data collection held a decidedly familiar resonance. As I watched these group leaders struggle with the many challenges before them, I often recalled my own early days as a basic writing teacher, sometimes empathizing with their missteps as I remembered times when I had wrestled with complexities that I only half understood. If I have felt certain protective instincts toward all the staff members who participated in my study, this was perhaps most emphatically true with Kalie and Morgan, whose lively openness was rivaled only by that of the focal students.

I have worked hard at being as evenhanded as possible in this account, juggling my desire to represent group leaders and other staff members justly with my primary focus upon the challenge of meeting students' needs. I write not as a detached knower but as an implicated player, as someone who has been part of this scene and others like it, and who continues to wonder what more we can do to make such campuses a place where all students are given optimal opportunities to explore and prosper. While I claim no "objectivity" for the portraits that follow, I can say that they were informed by an ongoing monitoring of my own biases and responses, and I leave it to the reader to judge their fairness and plausibility. My fondest hope is that these can be heard less as critical analysis of one program than as broadly based invitation—to think about one's own context in productive new ways, and to join conversations both locally and nationally about the role of educators in meeting the challenge of our growing diversity.

Endnotes

1. Responding to growing fiscal pressures and eager to provide college teaching experience for its graduate students, the department has since made English 90 an entirely student-taught course.

2. This individual was appointed Acting Academic Vice-President during the semester of data collection; the following year, after a nationwide search, he

assumed that post on a permanent basis. I refer to him throughout as the Academic Vice-President.

3. For consistency's sake, Susan Williams is identified throughout by her proper name; the term *CLP Director* refers to the individual who had held that post for several years and who was still officially director during the period of data collection.

4. To my knowledge, only once did a focal student deem a piece of writing too personal to share with me; this student removed the writing from his portfolio after the instructor had marked it.

II Responding to Diversity

Just how we are finally going to reconcile the entitlements and capacities of these new students with our traditional ways of doing things in higher education is still not clear. As we move closer to this goal, however, we will be improving the quality of college education for all students and moving deeper into the realizations of a democracy. Meanwhile we must hope that our enterprising new students will somehow weather our deficiencies and transcend our yet cautious expectations of what they can accomplish in college.

—Mina Shaughnessy, *Errors and Expectations: A Guide for the Teacher of Basic Writing*

3 A Commitment to "Educational Equity": Patterns of Tension

A Campus in Transition

Although Dover Park residents had long managed to keep nearby pluralism at least psychologically remote, during the spring of 1990 the signs were many that even this distance had begun to diminish. In April, *Time* magazine ran a cover story entitled "America's Changing Colors," and the eye-catching question "What will the U.S. be like when whites are no longer the majority?" beamed from every Dover Park newsstand. If the community as a whole did not reflect these changing colors, its university was at least trying to, and in the process it was bringing local attention to a national concern. The county newspaper was full of news about Dover Park University during the spring of 1990, much of it having to do in one way or another with cultural diversity. Lillian Roybal Rose led a conference entitled "Diversity: Unlearning Racism and Sexism," the Native American Student Alliance sponsored "Native Awareness Month," M.E.Ch.A. capped off Raza Month by cosponsoring a lecture by Latin American author Carlos Fuentes, and Henry Cisneros delivered a commencement address in which the challenge of demographic change took center stage. Tactfully reminding graduates that "though, to be frank, the student body of which you are a part probably doesn't reflect in a real sense the changes that are occurring in American society," Cisneros went on to point out that by the year 2000, 92 percent of the citizens in their state would live in a county that was at least 30 percent Hispanic, Asian, and African-American. "It's no longer adequate to say we must work together because our Judeo-Christian ethic teaches us compassion or charity for these 'poor folks,'" he charged, pausing in the midst of scattered applause, "because as prosperous as we are . . . this country cannot succeed carrying on its shoulders the burden of 10 or 15 or 20 million people in a permanent underclass . . . we are in this together."

A campus of a public university system with a statewide commitment to recruiting and graduating ethnically underrepresented students, DPU had begun to pay serious attention to such arguments—and, from some

vantage points, it would appear that this attention was producing fortunate
dividends. The day after Cisneros's speech, for instance, the local
newspaper ran a front-page photograph of a jubilant African-American
graduate; snapped as he rose momentarily in the midst of the ceremony,
the photograph failed to take in the encompassing sea of white faces,
leaving unqualified this image of successful integration. Indeed, although
the 1989-90 academic year proved particularly troublesome for DPU
equity students, mention of ethnic tensions at the campus was ostensibly
absent in the local papers. During the first semester of 1990, when many
DPU students were pinning brown-, black-, and ivory-striped ribbons to
their lapels—the appended message "stop racism at DPU" underscoring
the intended symbolism—local residents might well have wondered what
racism there was to stop.

While the campus's rate of equity-student enrollment was well below
that of comparable public colleges in the state, enrollment statistics
indicated that DPU administrators had made a start toward promoting a
more representative demographic profile. But while the campus was
becoming more pluralistic than the surrounding community, most still
saw the dividends of DPU's equity efforts as less than satisfactory in both
quantitative and qualitative terms. Although administrators were quick to
point out that faculty were united in their formal support of the equity
mission, all described a campus committed to diversity on a rhetorical
level, but reluctant to confront the thorny complexities of translating these
good intentions into efficacious action. The Academic Vice-President
recalled unanimous accord when the campus mission statement was
amended to formalize a commitment to "justice, equal opportunity,
fairness and impartiality"; on the other hand, he confessed, "whenever
we've tried to involve faculty in the question of education equity, we've
gotten compassionate but blank stares."

For those most committed to transforming DPU into an intercultural
institution, a place where ethnically diverse students might thrive as
individuals and interact as a harmonious community, the words of the
mission statement were urgent and real; but these individuals could not
speak for long about needed change without pointing to the many
controversies that hummed beneath surfaces, of the private web of
tensions undercutting the public slogans. When asked about the campus's
progress toward its equity goals, one of DPU's few African-American
faculty members commented with a sigh, "White folks are slow to
change"—then, perhaps not wishing to offend his white listener, hastily

added the disclaimer that "*White folks* is not a color, but a mental disposition." At DPU, where 89 percent of both the temporary and permanent faculty were white, those hoping to promote change often found such a disposition both rampant and intractable. After describing the many factors that undermined DPU's equity programs, one administrator voiced his suspicion that these entrenched attitudes were toppling the best-laid plans, leaving little more than empty promises and lists of attractive-sounding programs: "We're just throwing resources at [equity students]," he sadly observed, "and assuming it's doing some good."

In principle, "justice, equal opportunity, fairness and impartiality" are ideals easily embraced; it is unsurprising, then, that at a campus where it was difficult to find anyone who did not lean to the left politically, it was even more difficult to find anyone who overtly opposed educational equity. Meanwhile, at DPU and countless campuses like it, equity students faced not only the usual freshman challenges—the disorientation of being away from home for the first time, the struggle to contend with the demands of academic work, to budget money, to find a social niche—but also a host of additional hurdles unknown to the middle-class whites who so outnumbered them. Even as faculty and administrators embraced the rhetoric of the new policy, the "ideal place to live and learn" promised on the cover of the campus catalog remained, at least for some students, a yet-elusive goal.

Though ostensibly eager to reach out a helping hand, DPU's administrative and teaching staff increasingly regarded the campus's emerging pluralism as a matter of persistent and nettlesome concern. Pausing periodically to remind their audience (and, perhaps, themselves) that they held a basic optimism about their institution's future, all expressed a vague uneasiness, a sense of misgiving at the changes the campus was undergoing. DPU's equity efforts were suspended among a host of tensions, riddled with oppositions that sometimes complicated individuals' perspectives, and often placed various groups in tacit or overt conflict.

In conversations with faculty and administrators, the following themes surfaced again and again:

- *Among many faculty, the perception held fast that programs like the Comprehensive Learning Project (CLP) and the Educational Opportunity Program (EOP) were solely responsible for "taking care of the equity issue," an assumption the directors of both programs firmly discouraged.*

The CLP and EOP Directors remained steadfast in their insistence that they could not meet the challenge alone—that, indeed, the success of underrepresented students was primarily dependent upon the efforts of academic departments. Both Directors had conducted workshops and chatted informally with faculty in an effort to encourage widespread reflection upon the particular needs of equity students, and both spoke of their frustration at the limited response they had witnessed. Noted the Academic Vice-President, "The campus community, for the most part, says educational equity belongs over there, and they point to [the Student Affairs building]," with many faculty members assuming that they "don't particularly have anything to do with that, except being nice and nonbigoted." The Dean of Students, while emphasizing that educational equity was "a key concern" of his division, also stressed that "if we're going to succeed, it's going to have to become a concern for the entire campus." Added the CLP Director, "Over and over, we have said . . . the educational equity effort at DPU, it's not me, it's not [the Director of EOP], it's not the special programs—we can't do it! . . . It has to be much bigger than that, it has to be diffused through the whole university, if you're really serious about the effort . . . we're all gonna go down the tube or we're all gonna fly—there's no way around it, I mean everything's too interrelated, too interconnected."

- *Some key administrators who were otherwise enthusiastic about the equity effort complained that lack of coordination among the many avenues of support for underprepared, ethnically diverse students rendered such programs excessively costly and difficult to evaluate.*

As noted in chapter 2, the overlapping intentions of existing programs were often obscured by their tangled funding sources and reporting relationships. The CLP and EOP, often named as the "key equity programs" on campus, presented a prime case in point. (Indeed, whether they fully qualified as equity programs at all was debatable, since neither used ethnicity as a criterion, and a large proportion of the students in both were white—a majority in CLP, and a third in EOP.) Half of the CLP students were also funded by EOP, but coordination between the two programs remained loose and informal, a function of the EOP Director's magnanimity in sharing resources rather than any formal commitment. There were also striking gaps in equity support services; since both EOP and CLP served primarily freshmen, for instance, neither was extensively active in promoting long-term retention and graduation rates. In response to such concerns, an educational equity subcommittee charged with enhancing equity-student retention was developing a proposal to consolidate available services into a single unit. While the plan would seem to offer many advantages, given campus cynicism about developmental education, one subcommittee member was already anticipating the exclamatory chorus: *"Not* another *program?!"*

- *Many faculty and a number of administrators felt torn between their support for educational equity and their desire to maintain acceptable academic standards.*

Especially since DPU did not have a large pool of underrepresented applicants from which to screen top candidates, dealing with underpreparation and responding to the systemwide call for educational equity were of a piece: "We saw that by definition serving the academically underprepared was going to mean that we were going to have a lot of ethnic-minority students," noted DPU's CLP Director. Although the CLP program had been instituted systemwide five years earlier to assist "underprepared" students, a number of administrators reported that at DPU (as, indeed, throughout the system) the CLP was informally regarded as a primary equity program.

Since DPU had begun to allot some of its own resources to cover gaps in the CLP budget, the program had become a warming focus of campus controversy. "When it comes to budget time," noted the Dean of Academic Programs, "there's certainly a group of faculty that say, 'Well, why bother, if these people aren't ready for college, they shouldn't be here . . . They shouldn't be in college at all, or if they are, they should be at the JC.'" He argued that such a solution would not help much with DPU's equity efforts, since the transfer rate from the local junior college was dismal: "if we're concerned . . . about changing the look of this place, to bring it more in line with what we see [the state as a whole] reflecting," he maintained, "then we have to get those people, and to put them in the JC is already to lose the battle."

Concerned that the CLP program was an unmonitored "hole" down which increasing sums of campus money were being "thrown," the Academic Vice-President at one point organized and appointed a Remediation Task Force charged with drafting a report on DPU's developmental curriculum. When asked why the group had never met, he confessed his misgivings:

I realized that what was likely to come out of that was a very negative kind of report, a report that indicated that we had spent hundreds of thousands of dollars, and we had gotten this much success. And that that somehow wasn't going to be a constructive piece of information for the campus, because there are people on the campus right now who think remediation in general doesn't belong here.

Notwithstanding his strong commitment to educational equity, he held that not many "stellar students will emerge from the CLP program," that "every one of these students . . . we graduate is a success story, and we shouldn't be overly concerned with the ones who don't, because we know we're going to lose a lot of them." Along with the Dean of Academic Programs, he worried that programs like the CLP were creating a "second-tier faculty"—part-time, untenured, and underpaid, their jobs perennially on the line as a skeptical permanent faculty debated the value of having a developmental curriculum at all.

The EOP Director frequently offered a forceful reminder in the midst of all this contention—that the underpreparation about which everyone was worrying and arguing was a function of socioeconomic status, not ethnicity. A middle-class African American, he spoke often of how observing his daughter's passage through elite private schools had alerted him to "how big the gap really is," driving home the realization that "my kids in EOP will never be able to compete at that level—absolutely, positively never. Ain't got a beggar's chance in hell." While others routinely regarded programs targeting low-income or underachieving students as de facto equity efforts, he was forever pointing to the complex and multiplistic associations among ethnicity, social class, and academic achievement. He took especially strong exception when people referred to EOP as "the minority program": "I say, 'Time out—I'm a low-income program. What I see in dealing with a cross-spectrum of color . . . is income-driven, and I'm seeing the lower folks, and where we've failed them.'"

- *While a number of equity administrators remained stubbornly supportive of students whose academic performance was subpar, many faculty believed that those students who were not succeeding were simply responsible for their own failure.*

Holding that too many equity students were failing to respond to the generous ministrations of campus support services, some faculty argued that such efforts were taking the wrong approach. Those most skeptical of the EOP and CLP termed these programs' work with students "handholding," "a parenting kind of activity," and "bird-dogging"; these critics often insisted that students must assume full responsibility for their own success or failure, that they must be allowed "the right to fail." Variations on this theme were heard frequently in the campus writing program: one basic writing instructor recalled sharing her concerns about her students' proficiency levels with the freshman composition director, to which he responded only that she should realize that "we give these students lots of opportunities—and we also give them the opportunity to fail." The Coordinator of the Tutorial Center funded by the Associated Students was particularly vocal about the dangers of "co-dependency" and "handholding" in working with underprepared students—including those who had been recruited under the new equity policy—and stressed these concerns in the occasional workshops that she had conducted for English department adjunct staff.

While allowing that it is indeed possible to be "too helpful," the CLP Director argued that "a certain amount of handholding has to go on":

> that's part of the program, that's part of the developmental educa-
> tion system . . . part of it is you have to do some handholding, because
> you have somebody here who has some needs. They have to have
> their hands held as they go across certain crevices, certain abysses—
> bigger than crevices, you know. They have to have that; most of
> them are first-generation college, this is totally new to them.

Meanwhile, observed the Academic Vice-President, most faculty "haven't really changed their attitudes from the time when they themselves were students," providing lectures, a syllabus, and office hours, but announcing to students that "the job of getting through this course is essentially up to you."

Noting his frustration with those who hold fast to either extreme in this debate, the Dean of Students argued that an ideal response to *all* students—including underprepared equity students—exists somewhere between the extremes of "handholding" and "hands-off":

> I'd like to see people understand that there is a continuum . . . some
> students, when they first come to the institution, do need more
> intensive support, and I think if we're going to bring students here
> we do have an obligation to give them every chance to succeed. And
> that means they still have "the right to fail," if you want to describe
> it as that, by not taking advantage of the variety of support services

that we offer, but that over time, our goal is to create independent learners . . . but I see it as a gradual assumption of more individual responsibility on the part of the student.

- *While equity students often wished to preserve a strong sense of ethnic identity, many faculty and students expressed the concern that this might lead to ethnic separatism.*

A member of DPU's English department articulated a rather strong version of this concern:

> I'm an old-fashioned integrationist. And one of the problems I see on this campus [as elsewhere] . . . is the reluctance of minority groups to integrate, that they isolate themselves as a block and as a group. They own certain tables in the cafeteria, they congregate at certain places in the library. That's territorial. For example, there's a black student fraternity on campus. If I started a white student fraternity I'd be run off the grounds. So there's a certain inequity there that I think is preventing an amalgamation of the races on campus.

While firmly denying that the African-American fraternities at DPU (there were in fact four) had staked out areas of the library or cafeteria, the Associate Dean for Student Life acknowledged the ubiquity of the charge that African-American Greek groups were by definition exclusionary. He noted that such charges were being heard increasingly across the country as African-American fraternities and sororities had begun to attract record numbers—"particularly on many predominantly white campuses torn by racial tensions," according to a *New York Times* article (Wilkerson 1989). The Associate Dean for Student Life seconded the assertion of the *New York Times* piece that these clubs are among the most significant and well-funded of all African-American organizations. "Next to the impact of the church on the black community nationwide," he held, "black Greek organizations . . . are the second most influential entity within the larger black community around the country." A recent article in the *Chronicle of Higher Education* similarly argued that these organizations "have grown to be among Blacks' strongest political, social, and cultural forces, producing such leaders as the Rev. Jesse L. Jackson, and Martin Luther King, Jr." (Collision 1984, A34).

Both the Associate Dean for Student Life and the Dean of Students expressed concern over the power of African-American fraternities at DPU, suspecting that their considerable influence upon African-American students sometimes worked against the stated intentions of these organizations, particularly their pledge to encourage rigorous study habits and provide community service. The Associate Dean for Student Life also expressed concern that since much of the governance of African-American fraternities came from senior members off campus, his role in shaping these organizations—especially with respect to encouraging members' academic development—was frustratingly limited. Indeed, a number of administrators and faculty members saw the African-American fraternities eroding rather than supporting members' academic progress. When asked about such groups, the Dean of Students noted that they "provide a home base" but are also "separatist"; then he hastily redirected the focus to the integration-minded Inter-Cultural Center, calling it "a ray of hope in all this." The editor-in-chief of the campus newspaper expressed a similar perspective in his final column of the semester, arguing that "as long as there is a need for fraternities for people of color we know prejudices still exist," and urging students to explore the Inter-Cultural Center and take some courses offered by the American Multicultural Studies department.

"I don't think there's very much mixing between the races on this campus, and it's very sad," noted the CLP Director—allowing that students share the blame, but primarily faulting instructors for their failure to reach out to ethnically diverse students. While most faculty were loath to speak directly of the uneasy coexistence of the races at DPU, evidence of their quiet frustration often emerged in conversation. For instance, an English professor who had helped initiate DPU's basic writing program grimaced as he recalled his experience teaching the first section of the course. The students were "nearly all black," he explained, adding that "the first thing was a problem with motivation"—a failure to attend regularly, to turn in work on time, to envision the writing process as either rigorous or meaningful. They seemed to feel, he recalled, "a little resentment, that . . . this was being put on them, as though it's to deny their identity." Meanwhile, the EOP Director responded to such concerns by underscoring that the issue of assimilation versus ethnic identity not only involved campus clubs and gathering places but, in a pivotal sense, academic writing as well. While agreeing that many African-American students refused to "buy into" the sorts of discourse that English instructors expect, he traced such resistance to writing instructors' failure to build from African-American oral tradition, thereby setting up a situation where "to buy into [expository discourse] is to put themselves down."

- *Though upbeat about the efforts of their various offices, some admin-istrators worried that whatever success they might achieve in promot-ing equity students' academic and social adjustment was canceled by the troubled relationship between these students and the larger com-munity.*

"Our retention this year for black students is going to be god-awful poor," the EOP Director sadly predicted, adding, less prophetically, "I already know a bunch of them are leaving." At DPU, everyone seemed to trust that such oblique references would be readily understood, even though the series of events to which he referred had begun unfolding months earlier, during the early weeks of the academic year. In October, a promising African-American freshman, an exceptionally popular young man who had emerged as a leader in the Summer Bridge program, had been arrested for raping a white student. The incident received more play in the local press than virtually any event on campus all year. Without a doubt, observed the Associate Dean for Student Life, the ensuing fallout "tore the place apart"; added the Dean of Students, it "just pitted one group of students against another, definitely accentuated the fears and the barriers."

In the weeks that followed, it became disturbingly apparent that publicity surrounding the rape case was influencing community percep-tions about DPU students of color in generalized and lasting ways. During the first semester of 1990, notwithstanding the efforts of campus officials to emphasize DPU conferences and forums which highlighted the impor-tance of accommodating diversity, the local press was concurrently signaling Dover Park's growing unease over the university's equity efforts. In retrospect, the shift is clearly evident in the stories that the local newspaper ran soon after the sexual assault charge. Although no overt mention was made of the growing tensions within the DPU community, the crime page featured a story about plans by "angry Black students" to stage a protest rally and raise funds for the student's defense. The article, sandwiched between a piece about a fatal stabbing and another about drug enforcement, highlighted an enlarged, boxed quote from one of the accused's friends: "We came up here to get away from the ruckus [in our inner-city neighborhood], and look what happens."

In early March, around the time that local papers were running stories about the student's trial, an extensive, front-page story appeared in the Sunday edition of the county newspaper. "Gangs prowl for drug turf: inner-city gang influence moves into Dover Park" read the banner headline, beneath it a full-color, oversized photo of local gang graffiti. Interviewed for the article was a Dover Park police lieutenant who spoke of his suspicion that members of two notorious street gangs from elsewhere in the state had begun "intermixing and relating" with fledgling local gangs. Noting that nearly a dozen members of these gangs had been spotted locally, the officer went on to speculate: "Some moved here to get away from the gang influence. Some, we feel, are here for recruitment and some are Dover Park University students here on scholarships."

A group of DPU Hispanic students gathered soon after the article appeared to talk about their sense of outrage and to share tales of the suspicious stares and outright harassment that many were receiving from community members following its publication. Soon they were joined by representatives of the Black Student Union and the Asian Pacific Islanders Organization in organizing a protest march to the newspaper's headquarters. Carrying signs expressing their sentiments ("People of color do not equal gangs," "Speak fact, not fiction," "Educate, don't discriminate"), the group marched first through a downtown shopping center identified in the article as a prime loitering place for local gangs; there, security officers snapped pictures of the protesters, reportedly chasing one to get a closeup photograph of his face, cryptically explaining, in response to the group's insistent questions, "It's for our records." The response that they received from the author of the article when they arrived at the newspaper's headquarters was only slightly less vague, full of ambiguous gesturing toward "the growing influence of gangs in Dover Park" and insistence that "this situation cannot be ignored."

As they stood afterward outside the newspaper's offices, displaying protest signs to passing motorists, the group was heartened by supportive honks and waves—and heartened, too, by assurances from several reporters going in and out of the building that only concerns about job security kept them from joining the protest. The photograph that ran in the next day's paper must have been snapped after one of these happier moments: the protesters were smiling broadly, seeming more pleased than angry. They were, in any event, a small group of perhaps fifteen, and the atmosphere remained charged but never incendiary, the protestors too few and too well-mannered to provoke much concern.

Seemingly worlds away but close in spirit, hundreds of African-American college students marched to a rally across the street from the White House later that spring, urging political leaders to step up efforts to improve ethnic-minority students' access to higher education; Jesse

Jackson gave a speech, and the story made the national wire services (see Magner 1990). While the issues before them implicate us all, equity students at DPU remained "minorities"—a term most of them rejected, reminding campus Anglos that in the larger world, it would soon be their turn to try on that designation. Perhaps then, they suggested, whites would come to understand why, given the human propensity to pit "us" against "them," the word is infused with such alarming implications.

The Basic Writing Curricula: Good Intentions and Enduring Ambivalence

Set in place nearly a decade earlier after long and often heated debate, the campus's basic writing program was continually plagued by many of the same tensions that complicated campuswide equity efforts. The professor who had directed freshman composition at the time the program was introduced noted that while an influx of underprepared students had made the need apparent, most faculty held misgivings about "getting into the remediation business." When it became clear that yet another level of such assistance was needed, he recalled, the English department "wouldn't touch it," regarding such a course as "an added burden," "a really separate category." Seen as particularly targeting equity students, an additional basic writing tier was eventually placed under the auspices of the newly created CLP, which hired its own teachers and small-group leaders; the second-semester course remained in the English department, a few sections set aside each semester to receive those students "graduating" from the first-semester CLP course.[1] Though the arrangement had gradually gained reluctant acceptance, English department faculty continued to regard the basic writing program as a regrettable but necessary concession. Regular professors almost never taught either course, delegating these responsibilities to temporary part-timers and, increasingly, upper-division and graduate English majors.

A key gatekeeper (upon failing the course a second time, students were academically disqualified), the English department's basic writing course represented an important link in the campus's equity efforts. Since the course enrolled relatively high numbers of linguistic- and cultural-minority students, it also represented an opportunity for the department's faculty and majors (almost all of whom were Anglo) to encounter the complexities of diversity. The adjunct program's "collaborative learning" rubric shone with particular promise—that, as these "more expert peers" and their would-be protégés explored one another's culturally shaped ways with words, they would come away with enriched understandings of linguistic difference and the social nature of written discourse. As with the campuswide equity effort, however, such goals were more easily articulated than realized. While the adjunct program was informed by many of the same good intentions that had prompted a recent amendment to the campus mission statement, it, too, was characterized by patterns of uncertainty and conflict.

As I spoke with writing program administrators and staff about the role of the adjuncts, the following dilemmas surfaced again and again:

- *Teaching adjuncts should understand that the cultural and linguistic backgrounds of "caste" minority groups present (a) resources to be shared and strengths from which to build, or (b) stumbling blocks to be overcome.*

Expressing an abiding concern with equity students' levels of preparation and attitudes toward mainstream English, a number of administrators and faculty members suggested that one function of the adjunct component was to foster assimilation into the academic status quo. The professor who had helped institute the program noted that the small groups had been "pretty effective" early on, when they served a smaller concentration of equity students from poorer inner-city neighborhoods: "People who came in usually didn't have severe problems, severe handicaps in their backgrounds," he explained, "so small-group work as a supplement to their program seemed to be working." He suspected that was less and less the case, however, as the campus "began to experience the range of population of some of the city campuses."

"Most of the students in the CLP sections are minority, it's natural," noted a past adjunct coordinator, echoing the common tendency to associate inadequate writing proficiency with membership in a non-Anglo ethnic group. Many of these students both were underprepared and lacked "adequate socialization into the English-speaking culture," observed the Dean of Academic Programs. In adjunct staff meetings, the composition director often referred to them as "remediable" students, the intended note of hopeful humor resonant with campuswide concerns over standards. One basic writing instructor put it more bluntly:

> They were unfortunately educated. Whether they never heard what they should have heard, prior to college, or whether they resisted learning, or whether they were so confused or, you know, cut

school, or what, in high school, they are slenderly educated. They are ignorant, these young people are ignorant of the English language in its written form . . . if they would only forget their feelings about written English and learn it and do it, they would be so much happier.

Meanwhile, a controversial African-American professor who had once directed the program emphasized the need to move the campus beyond its deficit model of cultural and linguistic diversity, to encourage both teachers and small-group leaders to build from the discourse models that equity students had already mastered. Two of the basic writing teachers had begun to move in just that direction, and were working to convince the small-group leaders assigned to their sections to do likewise. One, for instance, had asked some of her African-American students to use the small-group time to assemble a class lesson and subsequent paper on Black English. (One of the students later remarked that although she had always thought of her native variety of the language as "bad English," the exercise had helped change her mind.) Another instructor saw the groups as an arena for student leaders to learn about the complexities of linguistic and cultural diversity—lessons which, in many cases, they believed tenured faculty were yet to master: "It's a real challenge to see these people as individuals," she noted, "and enlighten the faculty with whom we work that these are wonderful people with wonderful stories, and if given a chance, they can tell those stories on a very high level."

- *Small-group leaders should act as (a) nondirective facilitators, encouraging students to work with one another on writing, or (b) directive leaders, maintaining a firm hold on group dynamics.*

Although administrators and instructors often spoke of the small groups as opportunities for students to work with one another as well as with an adjunct staff member, most also revealed a concern that, in the words of the adjunct coordinator, the peer dynamic may devolve into "the blind leading the blind." One teacher observed that her students were typically so worried about offending one another that they seldom offered any feedback at all. When she had provided written guidelines to nudge students toward more explicit peer response, she noted their still "superficial" responses: "Like if it's an exemplification essay, I'll ask, 'Did the writer give three good examples?' and I'll get back, 'Yes, three good examples'" (cf. the comments of an instructor studied by Freedman 1987;

for a critical discussion of response checklists, see DiPardo and Freedman 1988, Freedman 1992).

Always lurking beneath the surface of such observations are fundamental questions of audience, meaning, and purpose; that is, for whom are students writing, and to what end? Should peers be allowed to respond as peers, describing their spontaneous reactions to a piece of writing, or are they to mimic the way a teacher might respond? As various individuals addressed these concerns, they revealed their perspectives not only on what it means to foster "collaborative learning" but, indeed, on what it means to nurture the composing processes of diverse students. Those who saw these basic writers as having deficient "skills" often believed that the small-group leaders should act as much as possible as surrogate teachers: the purpose of the adjunct program, noted one instructor, is "to take the burden of teaching composition from scratch off of the instructor." On the other hand, one instructor took a more egalitarian view, believing that the group leaders should encourage students' "conversation, talk about papers," jumping in only to "give input during a crucial time when there's a conflict or where there's silence for too long of a time." The composition director seemed to feel pulled toward both perspectives—describing the most effective members of the adjunct staff as "facilitators of group discussion," but focusing his comments in staff meetings upon how the small-group leaders might interact more productively with individual students, particularly on matters of grammar.

- *Small-group leaders should provide (a) nurturing, understanding support to students, who often suffer from low self-esteem, or (b) insistent, sometimes aggressive prodding to students, who are often stuck in the quicksand of their own recalcitrance.*

While both perspectives addressed the often-observed lack of motivation among the campus's basic writing students and traced its evolution to unfortunate educational histories, they offered markedly different views of how the small-group leaders might address the perceived problem. On the one hand, students were seen as victims of educational abuse, in need of sympathy and gentle encouragement; as one instructor maintained, while these students' confidence has been repeatedly "squashed by teachers," small-group leaders may yet be able to make that "human connection" and communicate the key message that "you're okay, and your ideas are very good."

Meanwhile, others tended to perceive these students as savvy decision makers whose avoidance ploys must be forcefully challenged. At a beginning-of-term staff meeting, for example, the composition director described the "typical" student's history of "copping out," "not turning papers in," or having someone else "correct the papers for him." When a small-group leader asked how to respond to one student's pretentious, "highfalutin" prose, the composition director urged her to assume the persona of tough taskmaster—advising, although group leaders had no actual power to assign grades, that she "give an F to every paper like that":

> And finally the message gets through—"Do you think you have to change yet?" You tell them it's a failing paper. That's one of your greatest weapons, by the way. The greatest thing they fear most is that they'll have to do this all over again . . . We really have to somehow crack through, break down that barrier.

These students are "not in the power of the English language," maintained one instructor, adding that "they either can't do it or they won't do it." Those who saw them as balky or lazy also spoke often of the need to remember that, as in the composition director's words, "We're giving these students lots of opportunities, but we're also giving them the opportunity to fail." Group leaders were warned to avoid falling into "co-dependency" in their work with resistant students, and to adopt an attitude of tough-minded detachment.

- *In evaluating the work of basic writers who are linguistic minorities, small-group leaders need to understand that (a) everyone must be expected to approximate nativelike proficiency, or (b) such standards are inappropriate to a linguistically diverse population.*

Many of the basic writing teachers emphasized the particular need for training which would better prepare group leaders to work with students who are nonnative speakers of English; often, complained one instructor, small-group leaders "don't understand what an ESL student is up against, and . . . they evaluate an ESL student the same way they would an American student, an English-as-a-first-language student." With tenured faculty holding varying conceptions of appropriate standards for evaluating the work of these students, a cohesive approach to guiding the group leaders' work remained an unmet challenge.

To further vex the issue, when faculty and administrators discussed the problem of evaluating the work of nonnative speakers, they often employed rather narrow definitions of an "ESL paper." For instance, when I asked in interviews about the writing of what I called "linguistic minorities" or "bilingual students," nearly everyone answered the question as if I had asked specifically about recent immigrants—nonnative speakers of English typically seen as ambitious and bright, but "handicapped" by first-language "interference." Largely sidestepped in such responses were the needs of the campus's "caste" minorities (Ogbu 1978)—those students who had grown up in the United States in homes where a stigmatized language or variety of English had been spoken. One writing program administrator conveyed this tendency when I asked what sorts of preparation group leaders need to work with "bilingual writers":

> First, [the group leaders] have to realize that the text that student produces is not an adequate measure of their intelligence. So often with native students we make that assumption, you know, that poor writers aren't, you know, aren't bright. We cannot make that assumption about foreign students. Oftentimes they may be quite sensitive, quite bright, but they just don't know the language that well yet.

While he clearly intended to communicate support for nonnative speakers, given his apparent belief that the writing of native speakers is a legitimate indicator of overall intelligence, the implication that only "foreign students" count as linguistic minorities becomes rather troubling. While recent immigrants were typically seen as having a legitimate excuse for their departures from nativelike writing, students who had grown up primarily in the States but who had spoken a language other than English at home were considered resistant or inattentive if they displayed less than nativelike proficiency in writing.

This pattern of assumption was again revealed when I mentioned to a campus administrator that two of the students that I had selected as focal students had been placed in a campus program for underprepared students solely on the basis of their writing placement exams, having scored quite high on the math test. Before I had a chance to explain that one was a speaker of Black English and the other enduringly troubled by an abrupt switch from bilingual to English-immersion instruction in second grade, he volunteered what he thought to be an educated guess:

> Foreign students. Typically that's, if you look at those, and then you look at their names, and you say, "Well, I suspect this student is Oriental," or from the Middle East, or something like that. It's not

always true, of course, but a lot of time, that's the profile, you see.
They come from a program that has had a tradition of having respect
for learning, and for things like mathematics, and yet they're having
difficulty with the language.

Similar perceptions were displayed in adjunct staff meetings—"immigrant" students seen as having "respect for learning" but "difficulty with the language"; "caste" students seen as less encumbered in a linguistic sense, but held back by attitude problems. When the focus was on relatively recent immigrants, the discussion rarely strayed from how to help with error correction; when the focus was on "caste" minority students, the discussion rarely strayed from concerns about motivation and leader-student trust. In neither case was the intermeshing between the social and linguistic aspects of students' academic growth explored, reflecting something of the schism that ran through most departmental discussions of bilingual writing and writers.

Since "caste" minority students who had grown up bilingual did not fit the prevalent ESL category, their linguistic negotiations were rendered largely invisible to administrators and faculties, their academic struggles written off to an obscure resistance to the opportunities before them. As Valdés (1991) points out, while such students typically confront a range of lingering linguistic difficulties—spotty vocabulary, inadequate control of English idiom, a preponderance of "fossils" from a native language—practitioners and researchers alike have tended to overlook these difficulties, focusing their efforts to understand "linguistic minorities" upon those still struggling toward basic communicative competence. Since the campus's equity students belonged much more often to the former category, this gap must be regarded as both problematic and significant.

- *In terms of preparation to work with basic writers, small-group leaders most need (a) a quizzical, reflective habit of mind, or (b) specific strategies and techniques.*

Debates about adjunct staff training provided a microcosm of the many tensions attending the writing program's role in the campus equity mission. Efforts to describe "what group leaders need to know" were enmeshed in larger patterns of uncertainty—concerning what it means to "teach the writing process," to promote "collaborative learning," and, particularly, to understand and accommodate students' instructional needs. Although nearly everyone agreed that the current training was inadequate (group leaders were requested but not required to attend two or three staff meetings during the semester), different proposals were advanced for improving it. While program administrators described desired facilities and equipment (a centralized writing lab with computers, overhead projectors, and a library of resource books), four of the five basic writing teachers interviewed focused their comments on the need to promote better "people skills" among the group leaders. Describing their interventions in a lengthening series of conflicts between adjunct staff and students, the instructors emphasized the need to alert group leaders to how their students' writing was situated within a larger process of social and academic adjustment. Noting that the group leaders "really translate into action . . . what we've set up as a kind of theoretical base within the classroom," one instructor returned again and again to what she called the "interpersonal . . . and cultural aspects" of their work. Mused another, "group leaders often don't know how to engage the students because the students come from such different orientations, and different cultures, and different socioeconomic backgrounds."

Meanwhile, the discussions in adjunct staff meetings were peppered with "tips" and "tricks," rarely straying from discussion of practical strategies for addressing specific problems—how to motivate the recalcitrant, how to help students find the errors in their sentences, whom to contact when conflicts arose that the group leader could not resolve. When asked how he would envision an "ideal adjunct program," the composition director allowed that more extensive training would be advisable, but outlined an approach which would likewise emphasize the practical over the conceptual. In what he described as "a formal block of instruction," he would provide "an overview of the writing process—prewriting, revision, and editing—and show them that's the sequence they'll be working with." The training would be organized around help that could be provided in each of these areas, he explained, noting that he would also model appropriate strategies and show videotapes "for critique—what worked, what didn't." Further, he would share an abundance of student writing with the group leaders, this "to show them the kinds of errors they can expect, and strategies for helping students solve them."

To those who saw the group leaders' job as "translating into action" what had been outlined in skeletal form by the classroom teacher, even this amplified training would likely be perceived as inadequate. Such a course of training would appear to sidestep many of the concerns that the basic writing teachers saw as key—training group leaders to be facilitators, for instance, or encouraging sensitivity to equity students' cultural and linguistic backgrounds. Further, while the department remained divided on the issue of how to address the writing of nonnative speakers of English, no mention was made of these unresolved dilemmas. Again, the tendency was to speak of the students served by the adjunct program as a more or less cohesive group, with attention to specific strategies taking precedence over quizzical musing or attention to the politics of linguistic variety.

Although administrators and faculty alike spoke of the need for more extensive training, many were reluctant to devote time and energy to the enterprise. Noted course instructor Susan Williams, "the group leaders need many things, but unfortunately I'm just not being paid to do what needs to be done"; similarly, two instructors who met fairly regularly with their teaching adjuncts maintained that this responsibility more properly rested with the program director. Despite instructors' calls for stronger leadership, however, the task of mentoring small-group leaders was largely left to instructors and experienced adjunct staff. Sidestepping hands-on engagement, tenured faculty generally believed that the small groups offered a generous degree of support, and that a shared responsibility properly rested in the hands of the students that the adjunct component was designed to serve.

Endnote

1.   This was the case with the course section followed in this research: it was a second-semester class administered by the English department, but it contained exclusively CLP students who had just completed a first-semester basic writing course.

4 Patterns of Tension Revisited: The Group Leaders' Perspectives

This chapter is about apparent contrasts and underlying connections—about two group leaders with markedly different backgrounds, aspirations, and approaches to their work, and about how their grapplings reflected larger patterns of conflict and tension. On the one hand, a close look at Kalie and Morgan revealed something of the human variation to be found within an adjunct staff often described as more or less homogeneous; on the other, to observe carefully as they reflected upon their work was to watch recurrent themes resurface, to glimpse in microcosm many of the same issues that pulled at campus administrators and program faculty. Placed within this larger picture, the group leaders' perspectives became part of an ordered whole, strands in the diverse meanings that together wove a totality.

While they began and ended at different points, Kalie and Morgan explored a common territory, confronting many of the same issues—about the nature of their task and, inevitably, about their students. This chapter charts these persistent tensions, examines the tentative resolutions that Kalie and Morgan had formulated by semester's end, and considers how their reflections upon their work were situated within larger patterns of institutional uncertainty.

The Group Leaders' Social Stance: Friendship versus Authority

Morgan

As she met for the first time with her five basic writing students, Morgan promised that the group would be more fun than work, and that she would be more friend than teacher: "I'm not smarter than anybody," she explained; "I don't wanna be real stuffy ... I hope we have a lot of laughs." In her log, however, Morgan wrestled with the sense of responsibility that she felt for her students' progress, describing her work as a trial run for that not-so-distant day when she would be standing before a high school

English class. Having worked in the adjunct program only one semester previously and having just recently made the decision to pursue a career in teaching, her anticipation of the coming months was charged with emotion: "I'm excited," she wrote, "but a little nervous, too." At twenty-seven, Morgan had arrived at a pivotal moment, a time when a new sense of direction was emerging after years of delay and indecision. She was thinking hard about what sort of teacher she would like to become, and her preliminary professional identity was being shaped in large part by her work in the adjunct program.

Some of the tensions that would preoccupy her for the rest of the semester first became apparent in the early weeks. In a beginning-of-term interview, for instance, she revealed a key ambivalence: "I don't like to come down as a hard-ass, ever," she noted, adding that she was trying to "get this feeling across . . . [that] I'm not any different from [the members of the group], except that I'm choosing to be real involved in my education." The afterthought reveals something of Morgan's underlying assumptions about her students' level of dedication, and the rather marked distinction she made, however reluctantly, between herself and them. Vacillating between the roles of peer and mentor, Morgan would often worry about how to communicate both sympathetic interest and high expectations, a concern that first surfaced in her log: "I see how it is important to somehow establish a warm communication with the students, but at the same time let them know that you have expectations of them to do their best." When a student described another group leader's penchant for wobbling off task, Morgan contrasted her own approach: "I never get off the subject, ever," she said; "everybody hates me."

Although Morgan struggled throughout the semester to be both a sort of friend and a sort of teacher, her emphasis gradually shifted from eager involvement toward cautious detachment. Full of hopeful optimism early in the term, she urged students to call her on weekends for last-minute help with assignments, reveled in the discovery that they sometimes knew definitions of grammatical or stylistic terms that she did not, and seized any opportunity to poke fun at herself. One morning, for instance, when a moment's rest against a chalkboard imprinted white lines across the back of her black jacket, she playfully vowed to avoid such mishaps while student teaching: "That's one thing I wanna make sure of, 'cause I don't wanna look dorky *ever*. God! I can't look uncool!" When Morgan mentioned books she was reading for her upper-division English classes, it was always in a low-key, decidedly unassuming manner—as when she talked one morning about *Catcher in the Rye,* explaining that she found it "really honest . . . you know, he wasn't pretentious." Similarly, she tried to communicate that students' own lives and ideas were perfectly acceptable grist for the writing mill:

> Nobody's comin' in and tellin' you, this is what you have to write about, this is the kind of form it has to be . . . you can just draw on your own rich experiences . . . and tell us something . . . and you've got a lot of insight, a lot of things to say, you know, share some of that, share some of your wisdom.

Later in the semester, however, Morgan's democratic vision and penchant for informal banter had begun to be replaced by a crisply professional air of purpose. Especially after she returned from the CCCC annual convention in late March, Morgan seemed to be groping for a more formal, academic approach to her work. Instead of responding as an engaged friend, she would often assign somewhat vague, general-sounding labels to students' developing ideas. "So you're getting back into the morality issue," she said to a student when he told her that he knew several drug-dealing police officers; to another, who was struggling to bring into focus a paper about ecological concerns, she enigmatically suggested integrating some "visual concepts" into the piece. "I don't know if I'm always honest in my comments," Morgan admitted in a final interview; "[I'm] just so much more teacher-oriented." While at the beginning of the term she had drawn a sharp distinction between course instructor Susan Williams's more critical responses and her own warmly spontaneous reactions (intended, she explained in an initial interview, to "show them how their writing affects people"), she later spoke of "adjunct and teacher response" as a single mode:

> We've got specific ideas of right and wrong, and better descriptions or better words . . . We have this richer background in the English language, you know, that's been institutionalized through education courses, and through, you know, different seminars and things.

No longer the informal peer who was "not smarter than anybody," neither was Morgan quite an authority figure. Even as she sounded increasingly distanced and formal, she often spoke privately of her sense that she was still reaching for a professional persona, that she had not as yet come to master the concepts behind her new verbal style. Morgan's grasping for a sophisticated professional vocabulary was sometimes awkward—a novice teacher's version of the basic writer's "interlanguage" (Kutz 1986), or, more subtly perhaps, registering an emergent, still sharply differentiated membership in multiple discourse communities. At semester's end, she occupied a transitional territory, her words communicating a yet-provisional sense of expertise and authority.

Kalie

While Morgan often described her uncertainties about her role as a group leader, Kalie spoke as the confident, well-established veteran: "I'm the senior adjunct," she was fond of pointing out, adding that with her three years' experience, she had worked as a peer teacher longer than anyone else on campus. "I get students that are harder problems," she noted in an early interview, "you know, because I'm more experienced." Twenty-eight years old, Kalie had had time not only to explore academic options and develop myriad interests, but also to become abundantly comfortable in her outspoken, rather eccentric persona. She was completing work for bachelor's degrees in both English and physics that semester, and was interested in teaching creative writing or literature at the university level; but Kalie had no interest in teaching high school or, as she emphatically pointed out, continuing to work with basic writers. Unlike Morgan, she envisioned a future career which bore little resemblance to her present role as a group leader. For Kalie, peer teaching was not a professional trial run but, rather, a way to earn a little money until graduation opened more inviting avenues.

Throughout the semester, Kalie tried to create a comfortable, informal atmosphere in which students would feel free to express opinions:

> I think that's one thing that does make a big difference, is the one-on-one interaction, the loosening up, the being able to joke and kid, and the being able to be honest about what you do and don't like about the writings and what you do and don't like about how you've written it, what you do and don't like about having to talk about certain things. Because then you can get in the small groups and knock the professor.

While Kalie worried when her students spoke of the lecture segment as "drier and more boring" than the small group, she admitted that Williams was more a "teacher figure . . . a little bit more distant." By contrast, Kalie tried to make her groups intimate and chatty:

I like to make my groups even closer, even less distant than some leaders do. Because I find that when I can get a fun, friendly group where I can crack jokes, and shock them, be blatant about stuff— 'cause . . . I'm a real person who would be interesting to talk to anyway, and I'm interested in your writing, and I write well myself, so people who are writers aren't all boring, humdrum people way out there. So I think that makes a difference.

Both in and out of the small-group sessions, Kalie presented herself as a model of intellectual audacity. Even as she stood silently in campus lines or studied at a library table, she made a few of her many opinions known via the collection of buttons, political and otherwise, pinned to her book bag—some reflecting her views on international relations ("Stop the bombing in El Salvador," "Peace With Nicaragua"), one voicing her opinion of the "Star Wars" nuclear defense system ("Hands off Outer Space"), and others suggesting her views on sexual matters ("I support gay/lesbian rights," "You want safe sex? Move to Iowa"). Iowa, it turned out, was Kalie's home state, and when I paused at the beginning of our final interview to read aloud the latter slogan, she felt the need for clarification: "They take it as a compliment," she explained, "but it's properly an insult." There was also a story behind the "Abolish Apart-heid" button—purchased, Kalie was quick to point out, from a source other than a certain street vendor she had encountered during a recent visit to Berkeley:

This shit guy in Berkeley, who's, like, the black guy who's the radical of Berkeley—and to be a radical in Berkeley you really have to be an asshole—he's trying to force me to buy a goddamn red ribbon for apartheid, to feel guilty about it. I look at him like, "I put on events! Why should I buy your goddamn red ribbon and your white guilt trip when I put on *events*?"

There was also a story behind the button that read "Born Again Pagan," having to do with Kalie's boyfriend's exploration of his varied and somewhat depressing past lives. As the conversation showed signs of meandering on indefinitely, I cleared my throat and suggested, "You know, Kalie, perhaps we should get started." She smiled broadly and noted with a touch of pride, "these are the kinds of stories I tell my students, though!"

Indeed, Kalie's group sessions contained many such asides about life and politics. At their first meeting of the semester, for instance, she began by asking the students what sorts of reading and writing they enjoyed, but became quickly sidetracked talking about her own work—how she'd written her first short story the summer before, a departure from her more usual poetry writing. She had decided to make the switch, she explained, because "poets don't make any money unless they get famous, like Ginsburg, and then usually they're disgusting." A few sessions later, she offered an out-of-the-blue opinion of the Coors brewing company: "This man—he owns Coors, right? And he goes to a black businessmen's meeting, right? And he tells them all that biologically, black men are just plain inferior to whites, they don't have the same brain power . . . I don't like Coors, can you tell?"

Although Morgan also talked about her own ideas and experiences, Kalie did so more often, and was less likely to try to help students make connections back to their lives and writing. Kalie frequently talked at length about herself, apparently assuming that her thoughts were sparking something in the students, but seldom taking time to ask what they thought. She often veered away from educational objectives, chatting about whatever she found most interesting at any given moment. When asked about the difference between her group and Williams's class, Kalie replied only half-jokingly, "I told more dirty jokes." Having briefly switched off the recorder on one occasion, Kalie could be heard explaining the need to conceal certain aspects of their conversation from my listening ears: "she doesn't know we bullshit, okay?" An incredulous student exploded with laughter: "We *always* do!" he protested.

Still, despite Kalie's ostensibly informal, peerlike presence, she too felt a certain tension between the roles of friend and teacher. She often took a rather authoritarian approach—ordering students to get to work, scolding them for waywardness, sternly reminding them of due dates and deadlines. When asked how her feedback on student writing compared to Williams's, she became somewhat defensive, arguing that her own accomplishments as a writer rendered her expertise just as legitimate as the instructor's: "What I know may be different from what she knows," maintained Kalie, "but it's just as good." While she did not seem as aware as Morgan that these tensions were a dominant theme in her work, Kalie likewise wanted to be both trusted peer and respected authority—leading discussions with the firm hand of a tradition-minded classroom teacher, but puncturing her own decorum with playful banter and provocative digressions.

The Group Leaders' Role in Motivating Students: Involvement versus Detachment

Morgan

Those faculty and administrators who recalled being immediately impressed by Morgan pointed unanimously to her vibrant enthusiasm—to her obvious desire to get others as excited as she was, to foster both academic achievement and enjoyment of the learning process. In describing her work with students, Morgan spoke again and again of her desire to be "like a really big cheerleader," a "positive rah-rah force," bolstering students' motivation with frequent praise:

> Ms. Williams . . . she's, like, the tough cop, you know. And she's gonna be really more strict with them, you know, and she's gonna have the right way to do it, "and this is how this is," and she has these things she wants them to work on. And I think I'm more the cheerleader on the side, saying, "Yea team, you can do it," and she's the coach . . . My way of working with students is based on a personal, intimate relationship with them where I gain their trust. I don't feel my strength lies in how many grammar rules and literary terms I know, but on my ability to praise my students and show them how their writing affects people.

On several occasions, Morgan explained that she knew her approach was working when students exhibited an obvious sense of engagement:

> When people walk away, and there's this urgency, and people are just kind of straining, and everybody's wanting to interrupt each other, because they wanna get their point out, and everybody wants to get the floor, 'cause they're talking, that shows me there's some good learning going on, if everybody wants to participate.

But if Morgan's standards and hopes were high, so was her capacity for disappointment. Ambitious and idealistic, she occupied the role of neophyte somewhat uneasily, holding her efforts beside a demanding yardstick: "it always really bothers me that I'm not perfect," she remarked in an end-of-term interview. Even in the early pages of her log she confessed to a nagging sense of "not doing it right," repeating the phrase "I hope I do a good job" so many times that it began to seem like a shield against creeping doubt. So, too, did she try her best to feel hopeful about the students: "The group of students seem to be very articulate and intelligent and motivated," she wrote after their first meeting, adding, "I bet they are going to produce some really good stuff this semester." Still, Morgan made it plain from the outset that she was also apprehensive about their levels of motivation: "How will I gain cooperation and really teach my students?" she wondered in an early entry, "and is it really possible for me to teach someone who may not want to learn?"

As beginning-of-term cordiality wore off and students' attendance and participation became a bit spotty, Morgan wrote about her gathering frustration and sense of rejection:

> I realize that some people are just really turned off to my person- ality. I am a very intense person, and I can be very pushy! It's not something I am going to beat myself over the head for, but it does hurt my feelings a little, but I know that is because sometimes I am entirely too sensitive. I am beginning to feel frustrated by the poor attendance of my group. And I also feel frustrated by the lack of motivation of the students. I really wish they would have their rough drafts ready on time! I know I won't give up on them, but I can see how I might just lose interest in the class. I feel like it is a waste of my time to show up when no one is prepared.

A model of feisty candor, Morgan was both puzzled and disappointed to discover group members occasionally reluctant to share writing or ideas:

> I hate it when people tell me, "I don't know," 'cause I have an opinion on everything, and I know everybody else does too— whether they voice it or not is a different story . . . it bothers me when people won't put their foot out—out there a little on the ice, to venture opinions and stuff . . . I get impatient when assignments aren't done, and we have nothing to work on. And then I feel like, "Oh well, I mean, you don't care, so I really won't care." Some- times I won't be . . . real focused when I need to be, you know— "if you aren't ready and want to sit around and shoot the breeze, I'll sit around and shoot the breeze" . . . but I feel like we're wasting time.

Morgan's manner of dealing with these frustrations shifted markedly as the weeks went by, signaling both her growing impatience and ongoing struggle with self-doubt. When Morgan found her group sluggish and unprepared in the early weeks of the semester, she was a prodding, only slightly aggravated, peer:

Boy, I'm gonna have to buy all you guys a cup of coffee . . . come on, guys . . . the strain and freedom of college life is too much . . . I know it's hard on Mondays, 'cause you guys are comin' off your weekends and all the wild things ya did . . . I know what it's like, I wasn't born yesterday.

As the weeks went by, however, she found it harder and harder to hide her growing irritation. On a rainy morning in mid March when only two of Morgan's and one of Lenora's[1] students had shown up, those present met as a single group. Beyond describing how disappointed they were at the day's attendance, both leaders seemed unsure of how to salvage the stagnant hour. Morgan asked about the guidelines for the new assignment and tried to get some brainstorming going, but to no avail. Finally, she confessed her discouragement and annoyance:

> *Morgan*: You guys, you know, I dunno . . . I'm feelin' like, uh, to have the three of us discuss this . . . are you guys gettin' anything out of our discussion? Or . . . is it not worth it, or do you just want to go? I'm sorry to be real harsh, but . . . I'm feelin' like I'm wastin' my time, you know? And I know that's just my particular feeling right now.
>
> *Lenora*: Yours, too?
>
> *Morgan*: [a tense laugh] I know it may not be fair and it may not be right and it may not be professional but . . . I don't understand what's goin' on here. Do you guys, like, have *nothing* to say, or you just . . . don't want to be a part of this conversation or is it something you don't want to talk about? You know?

By midterm, Morgan's "cheerleading" had become somewhat muted, and her manner more tough-minded and brisk. At the first meeting upon Morgan's return from the CCCC convention, for instance, one of the two students who showed up remarked that "it's sad" when so few were present; instead of voicing her own disappointment as she had in the past, Morgan coolly replied that she had decided to stop worrying about things that she could not control. Although Morgan remained intensely interested in doing her job well, as she experienced some of the ups and downs of the semester's work, she began to cultivate a cautious distance. In explaining the change, Morgan often eluded to a lesson she had taken away from a recent "Teacher Diversity" workshop led by the Coordinator of the Associated Students tutorial program: "I think the important thing . . . is to realize that I am not responsible for their lack of preparation, you know. If they're not ready, then it's not my fault. If they're not willing and motivated to work on the assignments, it's not my fault."

This is not to say that Morgan's stance made a clean shift from friendly involvement to cool detachment. That a tension was building between these extremes became clear, for instance, in her closing line of the semester, when she noted that the few students who had shown up were either departing early or working on other things: "So you're leaving," she observed, "and [he's] working on his psychology paper. Well, you know." While Morgan attempted to flick aside both self-blame and her own sense of disappointment, she remained in the end something of a frustrated and rather ill-treated friend. Even while striving to maintain a certain professional distance, she wanted her group to understand that they were not alone in finding academic life a sometimes daunting challenge:

> Group leaders should make the students . . . feel that we continue to be overwhelmed and excited and confused, but we're making it through . . . I don't want them to think that I think it's all so easy, or everything comes easy to me. I want them to know that I struggle just like they do, you know, and that we can all do it.

Despite Morgan's new refusal to accept responsibility for the students' lack of engagement, she still believed that a sufficiently conducive learning environment could lure even the most reluctant. She felt that her group had established such an atmosphere at times, and though discouraged about a good many aspects of the semester's work, she looked back over some of their more spirited discussions with satisfaction:

> I think that we know we had a pretty safe environment, and I like that, and that's what ideally I want to create in my classroom is a safe environment where these things can be discussed, and they can walk out of there, you know, feeling okay, you know, if you can bare your soul about some of the problems that you have, and that you encounter. Oh man, what an ideal.

Still looking ahead to what she would like to create for her future students, Morgan had become increasingly mindful of the distance between imagined ideals and likely realities. If she had not found all the answers, she had at least formulated some goals, emerging from the semester better able to articulate what sort of teacher she hoped to become. She had also identified a number of tensions to be explored and slowly resolved in the years ahead—how to communicate both personal warmth and high expectations, how to maintain credibility while displaying the messiness and uncertainty of one's own learning process, how to care deeply about students without assuming an undue burden of blame when motivation falters.

Kalie

By semester's end, Kalie was admitting freely to her own problems with motivation: "I'm into 'senioritis,' I gotta admit," she noted. Characteristically, she cast this seeming drawback as a boon to her work, surmising that her students had benefited from witnessing her unflagging persistence in the face of diminishing inspiration. In contrast to Morgan, who often wondered what she could be doing more effectively more often, Kalie consistently focused upon what seemed to be going well, and she was less likely to assume blame for problems or gaps.

While the pages of Morgan's log were replete with worries about attendance and motivation, Kalie remarked upon these concerns with detached neutrality: "Only L. showed up," "A. didn't come, but the other four did," and so on. In remarking upon one student's reluctance to bring in drafts of his papers, Kalie calmly observed that "neither did anybody else that much toward the end of the semester—that always seems to happen." "Usually in English 90 they're not that motivated," she explained in an interview, noting that group leaders have to realize that these students often experience more outside pressures than most students—family problems, for instance, or the need to work long hours to meet expenses. They are therefore "more likely to miss meetings"—hence the need to "show them how valuable you are," and Kalie's frequent reminders that "I cost ten to fifteen bucks if you have to hire me at [a major university]." Often, Kalie suspected, basic writers' academic troubles are the harvest of uninspired schooling: "if they're from a poor area . . . well, you don't learn anything in the classroom, you just survive it." Typically, she explained, such students put a minimal effort into writing:

> They write usually as short as they can, they write very stilted, you know, when you write you're supposed to do A PARA-GRAPH, look, a beginning sentence that introduces all—you know, all that kind of stuff. They get very stilted by that . . . 'cause it's easier.

Kalie's antidote to such hedging was to try to get students stirred up, to encourage them to find topics about which they truly cared:

Sitting there and going, well, you know, writing is real fun and blah, blah, blah, doesn't always do a lot of good. I try to find out what they're interested in and help them see how it can be useful for that. Sometimes I don't speak specifically about writing, but I'll get around to it eventually.

Kalie believed that "whenever you feel strongly you'll write more," and tried to learn enough about students' interests and backgrounds to "touch on those veins." She did her best to remain engaged even when students' interests collided with her own. For instance, while Kalie admitted that "I really think sports suck," she allowed that students' excitement could provide a useful foundation—provided that they did not get "too emotional" and "leave out details and explanations that the reader needs."

Although Kalie sometimes emphasized that the students' academic woes were "not their fault," she also spoke of the preponderance of "troublemakers" and "behavior problems" among the students in her group. Even in praising the participation of the three students who came most regularly, she glanced back to less fortunate encounters. "None of these students are as bad as some I've had," she explained in an interview; similarly, she noted in the early pages of her log that "It's fun to work with these three and they all seem to be having so much fun without being a pain or obnoxiously avoiding work." Kalie often remarked upon the students' amicability as if it were somehow unexpected: "I think they were impressed . . . and all cooperated," she wrote after a session in which the students listened to her chat at length about her enthusiasm for Harlan Ellison.

At her very next session, however, Kalie perceived the lack of cooperation she tended to anticipate. Another leader was absent that day, and several rambunctious students joined Kalie's group. In her log, she wrote of her struggle to restore order to what she had perceived as impinging chaos:

Luis and Carlos wanted to be troublemakers, Carlos wandering off most of the time and Luis giving me a hard time by talking with others and hassling me with snide comments. It might not be the greatest to swear or make sex jokes in the group, but it shut Luis up, cut out the two girls, Mary and Anna, from letting him talk them away from the subject and got everybody else to bust out laughing . . . I guess it all worked out okay. I think forcing everybody to come up with one idea in a go-around called those two boys on the carpet for not paying more attention, and got at least one idea in each of their heads for them to think on for their paper.

Kalie often pointed to Luis as a prime example of a "troublemaker," the all-too-familiar "attention-getter" who jokes around "to draw away from doing their homework."[2] When I asked her to say something more about such students, she provided a fuller profile:

> People who have problems with their English, either because they're from black ethnic families, maybe, or because they're from bilingual Hispanic backgrounds. They have trouble doing it, so sometimes instead of working on their actual problems, they find methods around it. They skip a lot, they don't have their stuff done on time, they're not handing their work in on time, or not handing it in at all. They distract the class with jokes, they want to be the center of attention. If you're the center of attention, and causing problems, they're not looking at your work quite as much. Because there isn't as much time to look at your work because you're having to deal with your problem behavior, you know. And coming in late, that's another big one . . . So you have behavior problems more often from them than you do others, because they have a real reason, they have an even higher level of a problem that's keeping them from doing good writing. And so they've got an even higher motivation to utilize problem behavior . . . [given their difficulties with writing] there's more work, and a lot of them want to avoid work whenever possible.

Seeing her students' lack of motivation as both ubiquitous and firmly rooted, Kalie felt that she could do little more than offer invitations and opportunities. In contrast to Morgan, who even in the end tended to agonize over students' lack of involvement, Kalie regarded the motivation issue with toughened resignation—wishing to preserve a certain dignified authority in her group, but otherwise refusing to see student motivation as her responsibility.

The Issue of Control: The Group Leader as Facilitator versus Directive Leader

Morgan

Having recently attended a number of workshops on collaborative learning, Morgan was looking for ways to assume a lower profile, to persuade her students to do most of the talking. As she confessed at semester's end to a nagging sense that she had not pushed soon enough in this regard, she also revealed a persistent ambivalence around the issue of control:

> It took me a long time to learn how to sit back more. Which is what
> I'm trying to move towards in asking people questions, and I tend
> to, I think, tell people what I want them to do, instead of askin'
> them the questions to lead them to what I want them to do.

Morgan laughed as she said those last words, but the uncertainty to which
they point emerged as important and lasting. Throughout the semester,
Morgan's vision of ideal group dynamics moved between student-
centered and teacher-centered paradigms. On the one hand, Morgan
expressed a disdain for leadership of any kind, insisting that in the best,
most "collaborative" groups, leaders and students talk "as equals,"
generating "ideas and viewpoints" to be linked back to work on writing;
in an end-of-term interview, for example, she responded to some tape-
recorded segments of her early work by remarking that "I think I just talk
too much . . . rather than listening to other students say things, it's like I
just wanted to lead things, kind of." In the end-of-semester tapes she noted
a positive difference:

> I've just been learning so much. And even looking back here, I can
> see a difference, a shift I made from talking so much to talking less.
> And as I became aware of that, you know, I dominate too many
> conversations all the time, you know. That's something I always try
> to do, I try to pull back.

Ironically, however, as she explained what she would do in the future
to prevent the familiar syndrome of "the dominant people" taking over,
she outlined a strikingly directive approach:

> I'd pay more attention, earlier, to different personalities. And not
> relying on people to raise their hand and answer. I, you know, will
> make sure that I actively seek people out to respond. "And Fannie,
> I'm asking you, what do you think about this?" "Okay, and Sylvia,
> what do you think about this?" And actively seeking them out to
> answer questions—and making sure that people get equal time, and
> to hold other people off, while this person, who may be slower,
> makes their comments.

While Morgan was sometimes yet another peer vying for the coveted right
to speak, she increasingly took on the power to confer and deny that right,
molding the small-group hour to the interactional patterns of a teacher-led
classroom (see Mehan 1979a, 1979b).

The extent to which Morgan controlled her group's dynamics varied
not only over time, but also with the topic under discussion. Some of the

most democratic discussions occurred on those days when Susan Williams asked the groups to complete grammar worksheets; since Morgan's students tended to know a good many more grammatical terms than Morgan did, she frequently asked them for help, resulting in leader and students wrestling together with concepts none had fully mastered. When the group discussed assigned readings or preliminary ideas for essays, Morgan often reported with a warm glow that "everybody was real engaged, and everybody had something to say." On such occasions, the group occasionally remained immersed in earnest argument well past the official end of their allotted hour—this to the chagrin of Williams, who complained that Morgan's students sometimes came late to the whole-class session. On other occasions, however, Morgan assumed an air of insistent authority, as when she spent an hour lecturing on how to write a timed essay, lightly dismissing her students' cries of boredom: when writing in an exam situation, she argued, meaning making takes a back seat to performance, with function following form—the form being in this case the five-paragraph essay, which she reviewed in full and unapologetic detail. "I'm not really wanting to get too much into the issue of what, what your opinions are in the paper," she explained; "what I'm looking at is the process of preparing for this essay, this timed essay . . . you have to come up with a plan of attack."

While Morgan seemed to have a rather clear idea of how she wanted to approach most discussions, she revealed considerable uncertainty on those days when students were to bring in rough drafts of their essays. In interviews, she insisted that the goal was to encourage peer response:

> I think it's helpful to get peer response, but only if everybody has their assignments done at the same time, you know, that's really crucial to group work . . . I think that students view each other as not having absolute knowledge like they'd do teachers, and like they might do group leaders. So getting somebody's response, who they don't view as having more power or having more knowledge, just gives them a different, you know, viewpoint, and maybe helps them think about things in a different way, or they feel that they might even be more vocal about what's going on, because, "Well, what do *you* know?—You know, you're just a student, so I'm going to tell you" . . . whereas with a group leader or a teacher, they might be intimidated, and think, oh, they must be right, because they're the group leader, or the teacher.

When pressed, however, Morgan confessed that she rarely encouraged the students to respond to one another, and that she tended to approach paper-response sessions as a series of one-on-one encounters between herself and individual students. Indeed, she noted that on paper-response days, she saw the group setting as less than ideal: "You get so much better attention one-on-one . . . In groups of four or five, someone's working quietly over here, and someone's working over here, I've got to bounce around, I can't do them justice."

On a number of occasions, Morgan also seemed unsure of what sorts of response to provide. In a beginning-of-term interview she explained that she liked to confine her remarks to whatever aspects of a piece the student selected, but over the course of data collection she rarely asked for such guidance from students. Although her choice of words sometimes seemed to signal a directive intention ("Okay, your turn in the hot seat"; "Are you learning anything from me?"), she privately acknowledged her lingering uncertainty:

> I found myself very reluctant to criticize [students'] work for fear of offending [them] or discouraging [them]. I also am afraid of saying too much, of giving the answers. What I would like to move toward is maybe giving a little more in the beginning in order to "show" the students how to look critically at their papers, and as time goes on I will ease off and encourage them to catch their own mistakes. I just got an idea, maybe what I would ideally like to do is maybe just write one directive after I read the rough draft. Something like, "Go through your paper and correct all the mis-spelled words," or "Go through your paper and correct all of the sentence fragments." Maybe that way, the students can learn how to edit their own work better.

Morgan's tentative goals were nearly subsumed by the myriad questions implicit here: Is writing a matter of "having the right answers," or does it involve a more subtle, properly social construction of meaning? How important is correct grammar, and when and how to address this aspect of students' work? How to guide students in such a way that the work of exploration and discovery remains essentially theirs? How to criticize without disparaging?

When Morgan returned from the CCCC convention in late March, she had begun to formulate a more deliberate response mode; for instance, she was asking fewer known-information questions, playing back and extending students' initial thoughts, waiting out silences, and seizing the floor less often. Still, "collaborative learning" remained in her mind another practical buoy—a strategy that was helping keep her sessions afloat, not a new way of conceptualizing teaching and learning. While she had come to see her tendency to "talk way too much" as a habit that must be broken, she had only begun to address the issues of why, when, and how.

Kalie

Characteristically, Kalie spoke to issues of group control not as a searching beginner, but as a confident veteran reporting her well-established practices. While the issue of control became one of the many road maps by which Morgan charted her process of transition over the semester, Kalie presented herself as someone who had long ago arrived, whose stances and strategies had progressed toward comfortable familiarity.

Although she noted on one occasion that she probably squelched group dynamics by her tendency to talk so much, Kalie was quick to follow up this apparent self-criticism with the assurance that basic writers need firm guidance—indeed, Kalie defended her far-ranging monologues by explaining that even when she was not talking directly about writing, she was trying to engage the students in some sort of intellectual inquiry. To nudge the writing response sessions along, she noted that she would often ask the group, "Well, what did you think?" but wind up talking largely about her own "related experiences" in the hopes of "sparking something." Like Morgan, Kalie had a number of misgivings about peer response to writing: "A lot of times they have a lot of problems saying more than the fact that they liked it," she explained; "it's really hard to get people to be specific." Kalie estimated that around one-third of her students were quite reluctant to listen to feedback from peers, a tendency which she saw as somewhat justified in that "they'll often say things about grammar that are wrong." She registered surprise when the two African Americans in her group occasionally gravitated to a distant table to exchange their writing in private; in a final interview she noted that this had happened only "when we didn't have a lot of time," but such was not in fact the case—indeed, these were occasions when the rest of the group was at something of a loss as to how to fill the available time.

To a much greater extent than Morgan, Kalie regarded her task as a process of transmission: in a successful group, she observed, the students "understood something" that she had been trying to present. Similarly, after trying unsuccessfully to talk with her students about how to write introductions and conclusions, she philosophically noted in her log that "some things hit them right on the head and some fizzle out like this one." Not surprisingly, then, Kalie tended to approach response to writing as a series of one-on-one encounters in which she did a great deal of the talking: sometimes asking a series of open-ended questions, sometimes pointing out grammatical or stylistic flaws, and almost never pausing to solicit response from the writer or other group members.

Kalie comfortably occupied center stage, whether modeling provocative eccentricity or responding to student writing. When asked what she saw as the hallmarks of a successful session, Kalie made no mention of peer dynamics:

> I know a session's been successful when students are bringing in their work, shoving it in front of my face, "Read mine first, read mine first," "I only need to see what you think of this," you know. When you sit down at a small-group session and you're going through it, and Christian's, like, going, "Oh, I made this mistake," and recognizing them before you have to point them out.

While Kalie shared Morgan's goal of enabling students to become increasingly independent, she saw herself playing an active role indeed in that process. According to Kalie, the group leader's job is to do what the teacher does, only on a more individualized basis. "Even in small groups sometimes it's hard," she allowed, "because when you've got four people, sometimes it's hard to get to everybody's paper."

Kalie often spoke of her best peer teaching efforts as "theatrical"—energized, charismatic, entertaining. In working individually with students, she explained,

> I can stay more focused, I can stay more theatrical, but sometimes I have more trouble keeping up my enthusiasm when I'm getting exhausted and low energy. Sometimes you can kind of jive somebody else into getting the energy in the group going and then kind of draw yourself in. And with one-on-one, you have to be the only one.

If Kalie depended upon the students in her group to keep things going, this reliance was not readily apparent. While she was not directive in the sense of asking only known-information questions or calling on students to perform on cue, Kalie certainly did most of the talking, displaying her ideas and perspectives at sometimes striking length. In their conversations with me, the members of her group complained only occasionally about such tendencies; more often, they described Kalie as both likable and a bit offbeat, smiling as they recounted her scene-stealing moments, noting that she helped them feel similarly free to interject stories and opinions of their own.

The Group Leaders' Response to Diversity: Embracing Pluralism versus Encouraging Assimilation

Morgan

At a time when successful African Americans were still a rarity at DPU, the campus was showering Morgan with opportunities, honors, and financial support. She was, for example, besieged with requests to participate in DPU's equity efforts—the Dean of Academic Programs had appointed her an equity student mentor, the CLP Director had spotted her on the campus quad one afternoon and immediately hired her as a peer teacher in that program,[3] and in the semester following data collection, she was asked to co-teach an ethnic literature course. During the spring of 1990 she was awarded a minority-student "predoctoral" fellowship which funded her travel to distant conferences and workshops, and she also attended a number of on-campus events intended to foster equity students' interest in pursuing teaching careers. Over in the English department, where African Americans almost never enrolled in upper-division courses, Morgan was fast becoming a legendary success story. Indeed, when I asked the composition director to identify particularly effective staff members whom I might invite to participate in my study, his first suggestion was Morgan, "our black adjunct."

But even while the campus was singling her out as a role model to other African-American students, Morgan spoke privately of her ambivalent ethnic identity:

> You know, it's just I always feel so out of touch, so much, with the real black experience. I mean, I don't have a real good handle on Black English, you know, I haven't been raised around large groups of black people. It's like I even feel uncomfortable sometimes walking into an all-black room—it's never really happened that much! *[laugh]* And so I think, you know, I've been here in [Dover County] since I was eight years old, I've always been really comfortable hanging around with large groups of white people. All my best friends are white . . . I just have a problem with people who are always making distinctions between black and white, it's just always a big issue.

Morgan's attitudes about ethnicity had been shaped primarily by her mother, who had encountered the sharper edges of racism as a child but remained somehow untouched by bitterness. When Morgan's mother had become ill with terminal cancer, most of the many friends who drove her to chemotherapy appointments and helped keep the household afloat were local Anglos, women she had met through community organizations and her job as a probation officer. A year after her mother's death, Morgan still marveled at their loyalty: "So it's just real hard for me," she explained through tears, "like to sit there and say, 'Oh, white people are really awful.'"

Morgan recalled recently saying words to that effect to her long-estranged father, whose reentry into her life some months earlier had been marked by vocal complaints about her having "too many white friends." After he accompanied her to a local party, for instance, Morgan received a letter in the mail:

> And so my dad wrote a comment to me, that he doesn't think I have enough of the black experience, that I'm too white, or I act too white or, you know, even the way I speak, you know. I go to his house, and all his friends are goin', "Where she's from? She's got an accent, like from New York." And he says, "Oh, she's just been around white people too much." *[laugh]* It really shocked him that I was so comfortable around all these white people.

Morgan's reaction was equal parts irritation and confusion:

> So I didn't really understand his comment, and don't understand what me being completely involved with just black people is gonna give me, you know. Or how it's gonna make me a stronger person. I think that, you know, being a teacher, it's more important to, I think, care about everybody instead of caring about one particular group . . . I can't join groups like Black Student Union. I think if I'm gonna make strides for black people in my life, I need to keep making strides for all people, you know, and just because I'm black, I'm still a member of the human race.

"I'm first and foremost a member of the human race": Morgan repeated these words on many occasions, often seeming to defend herself against an invisible chorus proclaiming her "not black enough." Even as campus administrators and faculty were watching Morgan's progress with proud appreciation, she was forever defending herself against those who would call her success a selling out:

Well, it's just that when you're a minority person, and you . . . don't strictly identify with just your race and you don't think that all white people are bad, and you think on a more of a global level, you just tend to get really kind of shunned by your race, you know? And if you don't dance the right way, if you have any kind of mannerisms that are not real black, it's like they think that you're putting on an act and you're trying to do something other than just being who you are, you know? And it's just really difficult to be in that position. Because you always feel persecuted by your race, because you're not—they just think you're selling out all the time. And they have names for it—you know, "Oreo," and they have attitudes towards you for it, that if you don't identify and get involved with, like, the Black Student Union, or whatever things like that, then there's something wrong with you—you're not worthwhile.

Morgan wanted to communicate to other African Americans that "I'm not selling out, I'm trying to communicate my own destiny here." She saw herself as something of a model success story, and was quick to praise the campus for all it was doing for her—and for others, she suggested, if only they would take full advantage of available opportunities. When asked what improvements the campus might make in its efforts to support the needs of its equity students, Morgan invoked her own example as evidence of all it was already doing well: "There's all these wonderful 90 programs, CLP . . . I just can't really advocate anybody coming in, and saying, 'Well okay, feel sorry for me.'"

Morgan acknowledged that the semester of data collection marked the first time that she had worked with so many equity students, an experience she was finding both enlightening and strangely unfamiliar: "It seems so ironic to say, but I'm getting more of a feeling of black and minority experiences and attitudes and feelings from this group of students," she explained. Even early on, she admitted her occasional frustration: "they're just real insecure . . . I think they tend to have this feeling where they don't really trust people, that they're so used to not really trusting people"; "they're just really closed . . . at this point, I feel like it's a kind of street-kid, don't-open-up-to-anybody kind of feeling"; "there's this chip on their back, and it's always there." Keenly aware of what she sometimes called her "golden child" status at DPU, Morgan worried that to some, her academic success might seem more intimidating than engaging: "How can I work with them without alienating them, or giving them this superiority feeling or something?" she wrote in her log; "and then it's like wow, how do they feel about white group leaders? I feel that I have a little bit of an advantage because I'm black."

The message of the program's lone African American was little different from what the campus as a whole had long been communicating to non-Anglo students: don't be bitter, don't segregate, don't worry about assimilation, use the opportunities the system is offering you. Morgan looked upon DPU's burgeoning network of African-American–only organizations with disdain: "I . . . see it as an obstacle at times . . . I think sometimes if you look for problems, you're gonna find problems," she observed, "and if you look for good things, you find good things." Her mother had often warned that "hate will destroy you," and Morgan hoped to communicate a similar message to students:

> As a resource I can say I haven't had a wonderful, easy life. I've had a *wonderful* life, but it hasn't been easy . . . and as minority or black students, I don't think they need to have the feeling that they're, you know, doomed, or that everybody's against them, or that they'll never get ahead, or be angry at all white people or segregate themselves off. I want to present a resource of like, wow, there's a lot of things we can do, let's put aside color and race, you know, except when we can get into any kind of scholarship programs because of it. *[laugh]* Use it as you can, but use it as a positive thing, and take advantage of opportunities.

Morgan often contrasted her positive experiences on campus with what she regarded as most equity students' inscrutable sense of dissatisfaction. The negativity, she mused, is likely rooted in "their other lives," since she saw no evidence that these students were being poorly served:

> I mean, as a black student on campus, I have *never* felt, you know, that I wasn't getting any attention. As a matter of fact, I tend to get attention sometimes that I don't even want, and I think it's because I'm really vocal, I'm real outgoing, I can be really charismatic, you know. I think that's just me. I don't know about students who aren't. I mean, I'm a go-getter.

Morgan was particularly offended by the notion that succeeding at academic work meant surrendering one's cultural identity. In interviews and in group sessions, she repeatedly argued that mainstream English opens doors and brings people together:

> As a teacher, my primary goal will be to educate all my students, not just my black students, not just my Mexican students. And . . . I have to speak a certain way in order to get educated . . . this is what I've

chosen. And if black students see that as dropping out, that's their problem, and they're gonna really have to deal with that . . . If they think becoming educated and speaking standard English means losing their identity, then maybe they have to reexamine what their identity means, you know. And I have reservations about people who feel that they can't become part of this culture and still have this other culture.

Everyone moves among multiple roles, Morgan liked to point out—we all talk, dress, and act differently in varied settings:

> I think of language and culture as games . . . you know, you can just play in and out of them real easily. I look at Black English like you could look at any other language—like you could look at Spanish or you can look at French or you can look at anything.

At the same time, however, Morgan tended to regard linguistic difference as a disadvantage that her students must overcome. Black English, for example, was associated in her mind with illiteracy and lack of education:

> I mean with the whole slavery thing it was illegal to teach, and this illiteracy and coming up speaking Black English, and teaching that to your children. They just don't have the background. So it is difficult, you know, when you're used to saying "I be," or "I fixin.'"
> *[laugh]*

Those students who had grown up speaking Spanish might produce writing marked not only by first-language influence but also by inadequate attention to the rhetorical demands of academic writing:

> Or something like Spanish, where instead of saying the "white house" you say the "house white." I think that, you know, that these are issues in their writing, and it creates problems. They aren't used to having to be this formal, or having to write in this way, or having to be so descriptive, you know, being such a careful observer of what's happening around them.

But meanwhile, because Morgan did not ask many questions about her students' linguistic backgrounds, she often assumed that those who were in fact wrestling with the demands of writing in a second language were simply unprepared or unmotivated: "It's just that you didn't get the background in mechanics," she told a student who had spent much of his childhood in Mexico; "these things are easily learned."

Her idealism notwithstanding, Morgan had a tendency to trace student behaviors that she found troublesome to negative cultural conditioning; in Morgan's mind, a male student was having trouble dealing with strong women because he was Hispanic, while the marked reserve of two young women in her group owed to the fact that one was Hispanic and the other Native American.[4] Even as many of these students were writing about their backgrounds with affection and pride, Morgan sometimes assumed that they came from troubled circumstances and could therefore be persuaded to regard school as an escape route:

> I want to show my students how they can create their lives and destinies, almost by virtue of the fact that they are in America, and they are in school. I want them to know that they don't have to be victims to their particular circumstances. Right now I'm thinking about inner-city kids, and minorities. I'm not going to feed them a bunch of bullshit, or tell them I'm sorry for them. I will tell them that I'm not responsible for what has happened in their past, but I can have a helping hand in their present and their future.

Even as administrators and faculty were pointing to Morgan as living evidence that equity students could not only survive, but, indeed, thrive at DPU, Morgan was increasingly reminded of the many differences which set her apart from the students whom she was asked to mentor toward similar outcomes. As I read through Morgan's log at the end of the semester, I discovered an ironic testimony to her struggle to come to grips with not only her students' ethnic identities but also her own. She had taken the log notebook to the CCCC convention and recorded notes and musings from those several rather intense days—mostly scattered fragments of professional jargon, but also a capitalized and underscored bit of commonsense wisdom that had obviously found fertile ground: "NOT EXPECTED TO KNOW EVERYTHING ABOUT MINORITIES."

Kalie

Like Morgan, Kalie believed that most equity students came from trauma-ridden circumstances which sometimes intruded upon their academic progress:

> People from the ethnic backgrounds who are in remedial classes are the people who have more problems getting through because they have more financial problems, more family problems, they've got

more personal problems dealing with interpersonal relationships, because they a lot of times come from broken homes.

These students need assurance that "they aren't failing because they aren't smart, but because they have problems"—that is, emotional difficulties that "need to be separated from academic work." Kalie felt that the institution should provide both academic and psychological assistance to equity students:

> They're probably going to need counseling more and go look for counseling less, because their culture might tell them that they shouldn't go to counseling, or they might feel ashamed of the problems that their family has ... the fact that they're from a broken family might mean that they have more problems with relationships. Everybody's gonna go through the boyfriend-girlfriend problems, right?—but what if, you know, what if your dad left your mom because your dad got hooked on drugs, and your mom got dumped on welfare, and a lot of stuff like that. You're gonna have a whole different attitude towards what relationships are like. And you might have, from that example, you might wind up with people who are using you. You might have to go through some real severe crisis things.

Kalie believed that she presented a significant resource to these students: "I can tell them a lot of the things they're gonna have to do to get around stuff," she maintained—because she had been involved in campus politics and student organizations, because she had successfully navigated the financial-aid bureaucracy, and because she had "gotten in fights with people who are prejudiced." While depicting herself as a champion of equality, she was quick to point out that equity students need to meet the institution halfway: "If they don't join in and take responsibility on themselves to fit in," she observed, "they may *not* fit in." Kalie believed that she could help equity students learn to "fit in"—by providing information about clubs, tips for getting along in the dorms, and strategies to help them feel "more comfortable in classes."

Kalie paused to puzzle over the fact that not all equity students seemed particularly open to her ministrations, particularly those African-American students who tend to be "prejudiced against you because you are white." Recently, for instance, she had stopped by a meeting of an African-American sorority to tell them about a film that would soon be airing on campus:

They were the most unfriendly group of bitches I've ever run into. And the thing is they've started an exclusive black sorority, no whites allowed. So they are excluding people, some of them as far away as the whites are excluding them. So you get reverse prejudice.

Kalie believed that separatist tendencies within the African-American community were largely responsible for the campus's "very uncomfortable" ethnic relations: "Some blacks blame all their problems on whites and literally hate them," she noted. Often, she maintained, these students were not trying hard enough to adjust to their new surroundings:

You have to go out of your way to fit in . . . you know, but that's true of everybody, but the problem is that a lot of times they'll think because they're from a minority of some kind, that they don't fit in because they're a minority, and a lot of times they don't realize that everybody has to work at fitting in, not just them.

Kalie saw linguistic separatism as endemic to both the African-American and Hispanic student communities, and regarded it as an important obstacle not only to campus harmony but also to the academic progress of equity students:

Hispanics and blacks, sometimes they speak in colloquialisms among their friends and among their social groups, and if they don't, you know, interact enough with other groups, they're not really gonna be able to speak better, and speaking better does make a big difference in how they can see their mistakes in their writing.

The problem is particularly pronounced with Hispanic students, Kalie observed: "they speak Spanish among themselves," thereby "isolating them from everybody around them who can't understand what they're saying," and exacerbating their academic and social difficulties in schools. African Americans, on the other hand, at least "speak in English, even if they speak with a severe dialect," but they still "consciously isolate themselves together into groups":

And they'll talk that way, and a lot of times when you get into a group, a clique, a lot of times how the clique talks and speaks and stuff like that will be how to prove things to each another, and what the peers will approve, and a lot of peer approval within black culture comes from, you know, speaking in such a way that the whites don't understand, and a lot of times putting down whites who don't understand. And a lot of times having their own music and their own rap and their own things going on. And their own way of talking and their own way of dressing, that immediately drops silent as soon as a white comes around. Not always, but this is something that happens a lot.

Kalie often communicated the conviction that those outside the linguistic mainstream were at a marked disadvantage. When asked if she could see any way in which her students' bilingualism or bidialectalism might be regarded as assets, she replied no, "the assets are real low because of the problems they bring in." She went on to detail the "ethnic problems" she often found in the work of Hispanic and African-American students, whose speaking and writing "have inherent grammar problems":

They get weird grammar problems. And it also depends upon the language they're from. Spanish has a certain type of set of problems. You can almost hear, when you read the paper, you can almost hear that person's voice; and they'll speak with the grammar problems too, sometimes. They have a certain type of verb problems, where they have trouble doing plural verbs correctly. Or they have a problem getting phrases right and using the right word to start the phrase. They have a lot of problems with that.

Kalie regarded Black English as particularly problematic:

Now, ethnic black students, there's a big difference, because they don't have the bilingual problem, they don't have parents speaking Spanish at home, but they're still very ethnic. And for whatever cultural reasons, they've developed their own way of speaking that's a subculture of English. You know, it's a sub-, you know, some people say substandard, I don't think that's correct, I think it's a subculture. And it's a defensive-type mechanism, I think, in a lot of ways, where it's like they're cool, they have their way of relating, it's like a key to unlock their group, and you don't have it. And a lot of them can't break out of that, to write proper English that's considered what is acceptable.

"If you get a student who is from a school that has a lower percentage of blacks, or lower percentage of ethnic groups, then sometimes it can be better," she allowed. Still, Kalie explained, if such students are to maintain their hold on mainstream English and their commitment to academic work, they must resist the temptation to "hang out more with black students for, you know, community feeling." While Morgan saw mainstream English as an expedient variety of the language, Kalie seemed to see it as intrinsically better: Black English, she explained, "isn't as correct [as mainstream English] when it's written down . . . it's not going to make it . . . when you get into certain teachers that are going to demand a higher academic style."[5]

When I asked Kalie if she had any special training which prepared her to work with linguistic minorities, she interpreted the question as a token of admiration: "No," she explained, breaking into a wide smile, "I just started doing it, and I've worked with people enough, you know, I lost count, maybe ten different language backgrounds, not just Spanish." I pressed further: what precisely had she learned? "I've learned about different cultures," she replied, "a lot of stuff about different grammar problems and grammar patterns from different cultures." Perhaps Kalie's attitudes were born of a desire to see these students succeed in the mainstream, but her outlook was undercut by a less fortunate, less conscious ethnocentrism. In any case, as the semester drew to a close, she continued to worry aloud about the disfiguring imprint of "severe dialects" and "ethnic problems" in her students' writing—her expansive, free-spirited outlook consistently absent from her musings upon linguistic diversity, an area where she continued to see more problems to be solved than opportunities to be embraced.

Group Leaders' Perspectives on Training: The Desire for Autonomy versus the Need for Expertise

Morgan

Morgan remembered feeling "real apprehensive" during her first weeks as a group leader, and wished that she had been given some "written goals and objectives" to guide her work. She had found the staff meetings to be less than helpful: "once in a while someone would bring up classroom issues," she recalled, noting that the discussions were typically long on logistics and short on substance. Morgan had asked the composition director for a copy of the resource book that he made available to new staff (Meyer and Smith's *The Practical Tutor,* 1987), but she had only scanned it, and never sought out the composition director or adjunct coordinator to talk over what she read about or encountered in her work with students. What Morgan had found most useful during that first semester was talking to a friend who happened to be a program veteran—an empathetic, trusted peer who was a good listener and occasional dispenser of sage advice.

While Morgan allowed that "a little bit of training time" would have been helpful, she did not envision a semester-long class: "It would be really important to have maybe one or two . . . two-hour, or three-hour workshops," she mused, adding that "I don't think it's necessary to have a class that you have to work with every day, or once a week." Just as she grumbled in her log about all the "bullshit" one had to go through to earn a teaching credential, Morgan also regarded extensive training as an undue inconvenience, an added infringement upon her already crowded schedule. She was fairly happy with the autonomy that the program was providing her—room to seek out whatever sorts of expertise or advice that seemed most useful at a given moment, room to work unobserved with a small group of students who were hers for the semester. Although she did not mind talking with the friends whom she chose to approach, she balked at the idea of having to share her work with supervisors or colleagues at large. She often noted her aversion to the intrusions of fellow staff members: "I found myself slightly irritated today when another leader contradicted a response I gave to a student," she wrote in the early pages of her log; "I find that I much prefer to work with a small group of students without other adjuncts present."

But by the end of her rather challenging spring semester, Morgan was a bit more open to the idea of instituting some sort of initial preparation and ongoing guidance. On the one hand, she still felt that adjunct staff should determine the amount and nature of whatever training they were to receive, holding sole power to call meetings and set agendas. On the other hand, she often invoked the Associated Students' tutorial program—which required that all new staff members enroll in a semester-long class—as a potential model. Initially, the A.S. training commitment had struck her as excessive: "I thought, 'I'm gonna have to do this, and also be enrolled in a class!?' I was really turned off to it." Having worked for two semesters in a program without formal training, however, she had since come around to seeing certain benefits in the A.S. policy—"if only," she allowed, "it wasn't so rigid." But when asked to describe a more appropriate approach, Morgan was uncertain: "If I only had meetings like . . . once or twice a month, bitch session, you know, you just show up if you want to. But then again, who's gonna show up, you know?"

Not only was Morgan unsure of how much training should be required; she was also uncertain of what its nature might be. Student motivation had emerged as an absorbing and vexing concern for Morgan, and she particularly longed for support in managing her growing sense of frustration. Indeed, this was what she had found most useful in the A.S. workshops that she had attended, sessions which had emphasized ways to avoid "peer-teacher co-dependency":

> I think that group leaders should have, you know, a couple of meetings . . . some of the stuff in [the A.S.] program, the brief exposure I had to it, and videotapes, I think were really productive. After I saw some of those, I came back thinking, "wow," you know? When students come in and they wanna talk about a lot of their problems, you know, a lot of times I used to listen to them, because I thought that was kind of more my role, and I'm realizing it's not.

While she still felt that group leaders should be encouraging "cheerleaders," Morgan had also come to believe that a certain tough-mindedness must be cultivated. In workshops, she mused, the composition director should talk about "what we know have been problems in the past with students," and should detail strategies for approaching sticky interpersonal situations with firm decisiveness. Group leaders must avoid backing students "into a corner," since "when you put students on the spot, and put it in a win-or-lose situation, then as a teacher, as an adjunct, you're almost always gonna lose." What group leaders need, explained Morgan, is a quiet, strong willingness to place responsibility for behavior and learning back upon the students.

Although Morgan had struggled over the semester with a range of complex issues—how much direction to provide her group, how to address the needs of her linguistically and culturally varied students, how to respond to student writing—in commenting upon training, she focused almost exclusively upon learning to maintain calm authority in the face of students' wayward behavior. Even as she listened hungrily for ideas and guidance, she remained suspicious that a course would represent an undue burden, robbing her of the freedom to feel her own way through the many dilemmas attending her work with basic writers. For Morgan, her impatience with requirements and her longing for autonomy seemed to diminish the power and complexity of her own rich experience.

Kalie

Kalie also remarked upon the insufficiency of current training efforts:

> They don't really have any training here . . . no, no . . . They try to have paid adjunct groups, you know, or, adjunct meetings, paid adjunct meetings. But they don't have them very often, but the thing is that I don't think there's enough encouragement to get new group

leaders hooked up with older group leaders who have ideas of how to deal with things.

Kalie saw herself as an underutilized resource: although she noted that other adjuncts came to her often with questions and concerns ("because I've been a peer teacher more than anybody else on campus at this point"), she felt that there should be a more formal network whereby new staff could be paid to meet one or two hours each week with a senior group leader.

Noting that she had "dealt with many different sorts of problems," Kalie seconded Morgan's conviction that "interpersonal skills" are foremost. In describing the sorts of expertise that group leaders need, she returned again and again to the problem of student "troublemakers"— "difficult people" who have learned "how to manipulate." New group leaders should be given a list of senior staff members' phone numbers, she suggested, so that they would have someone to call as problems came up. She also saw a benefit in holding occasional staff meetings—if, that is, experienced group leaders were present to give advice to newer staff members. Indeed, in the two adjunct meetings held during data collection, Kalie did just that, peppering the discussion with suggested strategies ("so it's tricks like that") as the others nodded in accord.

Although Kalie saw the need for more networking among experienced and new staff, she was basically content with the approach that the current composition director was taking. She held that the "bit of a yo-yo" who had briefly assumed charge of the program a few semesters earlier "didn't know how to use the resources he had," and had intruded upon group leaders' autonomy by insisting upon a nondirective approach. "You need to encourage different ideas," Kalie maintained, noting that "the best adjuncts care passionately about their students" and must be allowed "their own ideas." For this same reason, Kalie hotly rejected the approach of the Coordinator of the Associated Students tutorial program, who "picks people who are going to be submissive to her," encouraging a low-profile, reflective-listening mode of peer teaching.

"Classes," argued Kalie, "don't seem to do a shit worth of good." She saw herself, on the other hand, as rich in the sort of knowledge new staff members most needed—that is, a collection of strategies for responding to writing and, particularly, for warding off would-be troublemakers. Kalie's definition of what group leaders need to know did indeed assume an influential role in adjunct staff meetings, filling a void, however problematically, with such "tips" and "tricks."

Missing the Mark: The Group Leaders' Role in Promoting "Educational Equity"

Key players in DPU's equity effort, both group leaders underestimated the importance and complexity of their work, simplifying its contours and minimizing its rich tensions and challenges. While Kalie seldom ventured outside the stance of established expert, Morgan was at her best when she moved toward problematizing her task—worrying aloud about uncertainties, setting goals that she knew she would not reach, becoming curious about her students' past experiences and current challenges. In public, however, both group leaders presented themselves as seasoned dispensers of established wisdom, succumbing to the temptation to use the program's occasional "troubleshooting" meetings as opportunities to display their expertise. So, too, did most of their colleagues: again and again, adjunct staff who had privately confided their agonized uncertainties were suddenly transformed into unmitigated successes, unraveling tales of "what works for me." Understandably hungry for "how to's," few had developed a critical filter through which to sift these bits and pieces of prevailing wisdom, rushing toward answers before they had adequately formulated the questions.

In their desire to ward off criticisms or challenges, to deny the inevitability of self-doubt, Morgan and Kalie both exemplified the vulnerability of beginning educators. It takes time and confidence to regard such doubts as part and parcel of effective teaching, to learn to weather the vicissitudes of the process with steadiness and flexibility, to develop the degree of self-trust that renders self-analysis possible. Those new to the challenge need solid, conceptually grounded pointers to help them get started, but they also need to be nudged toward the realization that the best teaching is endlessly restless, searching, uneven, messy. They need encouragement to see that their own uncertainty need not be concealed behind a mask of serene accomplishment—that it can, rather, become the raw material for a career-long habit of intellectually rigorous reflection.

If the group leaders were insufficiently curious about their students, so too were program faculty and administrators insufficiently curious about Kalie and Morgan. Although many instructors and administrators had vaguely praised their work, no one seemed to know anything specific about their ideas, approaches, or struggles. No one knew, for instance, that Kalie took a highly directive approach, or that beneath her freewheeling persona lurked conservative perspectives on linguistic difference; and no one knew that Morgan was a different sort of African American than the inner-city students so eagerly assigned to her, that she was earnestly grappling with her own ethnic ambivalence and engaged in a trying struggle to counter the accusation that her academic success denoted cultural betrayal. With the themes and subthemes of the group leaders' work rendered invisible, no one could trace—for the adjunct staff or themselves—how these were woven into a larger process of institutional transition.

While the group leaders were occasionally provided tips and isolated strategies, what they needed was much more fundamental, defying coverage in an occasional workshop or staff meeting: that is, they needed a conceptual shift, a movement away from regarding their task as a collection of discrete "how to's," toward a theoretically grounded view of their job's many complexities and unresolved tensions. Such a transformation would require considerably more than programmatic reforms or innovations, demanding, rather, that the institutional context be transformed into a place where such rigor is pervasive, where commitment to equity students occasions ongoing reflection, where novice educators are generously supported and challenged. While there was much talk of how to enhance DPU's equity effort, little attention was directed toward the daily dynamics of particular services. For the group leaders and campus alike, in these basic writing adjunct sessions rested a powerful opportunity to observe such dynamics, to admire the densely webbed challenge of program and policy.

Endnotes

1. As explained in chapter 2, Lenora was the third group leader assigned to Susan Williams's course section, but was not selected as a focal leader.

2. Ironically, Luis proved to be one of the most conscientious students in the class, bringing rough drafts to the group meetings more often than any of the others and turning in work to his course instructor, Susan Williams, on a regular and timely basis. Lenora, his first group leader, shared Kalie's negative view of Luis; Morgan, however, who became his group leader at midterm, believed that he only needed a little extra attention and praise.

3. As noted in chapter 2, the English department and CLP maintained separate basic writing programs and adjunct staffs. Morgan worked in both programs.

4.   For an extended discussion of the latter two cases, see chapters 5, "Sylvia," and 6, "Fannie."

5.   While faculty and group leaders alike often alluded to African-American students' insisting upon "writing in their own language," M. Farr Whiteman (1981) has shown that such students may be keenly aware of the more stigmatized aspects of Black English and make a conscious effort to write in the mainstream variety of the language. This was the case with Al, one of the focal students in this study, who is discussed in chapter 7.

III The Students

Perhaps we would do better if we had good big words like the educated people. But we didn't. We had to say something was like something else, and whatever we said didn't convey all that we felt. We wouldn't dare tell anybody what we had talked about. People who were sure of what they were saying and who had the right words to use could do that. They could talk to others. And even if they didn't feel what they were saying, it didn't matter. They had the right words. Language was a kind of passport. You could go where you like if you had a clean record. You could say what you like if you knew how to say it.

—George Lamming, *In the Castle of My Skin*

5 Sylvia

Cultural and Linguistic Background

Sylvia's family immigrated from Mexico when she was eight months old, settling in a prosperous, traditionally Anglo farming community that was then in a process of demographic transformation. While Sylvia recalled that some of the local Anglos "began to hate the idea that Latinos might take over," the town gradually became a place where families from widely varied backgrounds peaceably coexisted. She seemed particularly eager to dispel any suspicion that it was an impoverished ghetto:

> The town where I live is an urban area, and it's middle class, upper-middle class. There is the lower class, but I mean, I don't see it, because I'm not around it all the time and stuff. It's not *that* bad. I grew up with, I don't know, a variety of people, you know, Mexicans, blacks, Asians, whatever.

Sylvia's parents had never become fully proficient in English, and Spanish remained the language of home: "they've picked up a little English here and there," she explained, "but like fluently, no." Although both held relatively low-paying jobs—her father working in the fields and her mother doing housecleaning and childcare—they had managed to purchase some lucrative farmland, send money home to relatives, and save for Sylvia's education.[1] Still, as Sylvia explained in an essay entitled "My Dream," she "felt sorry" for her parents, who "didn't have the opportunity to make choices" that she now possessed:

> When they were my age, times were hard for them and life was pretty much planned out for them ... Well, in this day and age I have choices. I can go to college, or I could quit school altogether and work. It is my decision. I also have the choice of the field to go into. I could be an engineer, a teacher, or a mathematician. It is entirely up to me. The jobs are out there, I just have to choose which one I will pursue.

Elsewhere in the essay, Sylvia explained that while her own life was already rather different from her parents', she would always share their commitment to family: "my family would be the most important thing in my life," she wrote, "because they will always be there for me, and they will always stand beside me."

But already, Sylvia's dual commitment to family and worldly achievement was fraught with paradox. Even as her parents boasted of their daughter's presence at a four-year college, they worried that she was losing touch with her roots; and even as Sylvia was trying to recapture an earlier sense of ethnic identity, she longed to break away from the typecasting that had long plagued her, to be perceived "just like any other American." In one of her essays she described the "many barriers" that she had crossed, the "many negative messages" that she had overcome:

> ... my family back in Mexico is proud that I am going to school, but some members put me down. They can not understand that I am doing something worthwhile with my life. They feel that I should do things the traditional way, which is to stay home until I get married. My family sees me as an independent woman that left home and will never get married.

Although Sylvia's parents had helped force her to take the first big step into the Anglo world—when they sent her, then a five-year-old girl who could speak only Spanish, to a local kindergarten—they had ample cause to regret her cultural and linguistic estrangement. The problem first became evident during Sylvia's second-grade year, when she made an abrupt and disruptive switch from a bilingual classroom to an English-immersion program. For a time, she was gripped with "the fear of speaking in either English or Spanish," and had trouble communicating at home and school alike:

> So by the time they said, "Well, here's English," I was like, "Whoa, wait a minute, slow down here!" It was just like a big switch, it was kind of hard for me. And ever since then I've had that [writer's] block kinda thing . . . I didn't even know the basics of my own language, you know, when they said, "Boo, here's English." You know. And the funny thing is, I *lost* my Spanish. I couldn't speak it no more. And you know, my parents, it was a really . . . *[exasperated sigh]* it was so tough to communicate.

"I lost it," she repeated softly, as if still amazed that such a thing could happen. "I could have lost it completely," she added, "and not even speak Spanish right now, and really be called 'coconut.'"[2]

Deeply concerned, Sylvia's parents arranged a month's stay in Mexico between her second- and third-grade years—this in the hopes that she might recover the ability to speak her native language, and might also realize the link it represented to her extended family. Sylvia found the experience disorienting and somewhat disturbing: even as she basked in the warmth of her relatives' hugs and eager chatter, she was literally speechless. At first, her brother was her translator and emissary—then, as Sylvia recalled, "reality hit. I said [to myself], 'You've gotta learn it.'" At first, she was halting and awkward, but by the end of that pivotal month she was once again comfortable speaking Spanish to relatives and Hispanic friends. Even as Sylvia approached young adulthood, Spanish remained the language spoken at home, especially when one of her parents was present—"to show respect," as her father had always said.

Sylvia remained apprehensive, however, about her ability to communicate in Spanish with strangers: "My fear," she explained, "is that I cannot pronounce the words and they won't know what I'm talking about." While she felt somewhat uncertain about her English writing, she was even more insecure about composing in her native language: "I just can't write it properly," she maintained. Flicking aside playful criticism from non-Spanish-speaking friends, she had futilely scanned the schedule of classes for a course that would help her speak and read her native language with renewed confidence. Sylvia spoke longingly of her nine-year-old sister back home: "she can speak better Spanish than I can," she explained, "and that's because they speak it in the house all the time."

Sylvia felt fully competent in neither language—in both, she was keenly aware of her foreigner's accent and uneasy about her abilities as a writer. It would be inadequate to say that Sylvia had made an incomplete transition from Spanish to English, the reality being vastly more complex, more tangled with dilemma. As Sylvia described her sense of being caught between languages, she inevitably described her sense of being caught between cultures as well: "It's funny, because like when I go to Mexico, I don't feel I'm part of them. I don't feel any less, either. It's just like I have two different cultures in me, but I can't choose."

While she felt more at home in the States than in her native Mexico, Sylvia was as concerned about recovering a sense of her family's culture as she was about retaining her first language: "I don't know my culture that well, to tell you the truth. I know more American culture than I know about my own. But everyday I'm learning, you know, and I like it . . . my friend is always joking with me, saying, 'You're not a real Mexican.' I say, 'But a proud one, though.'"

Although Sylvia's path had been far from easy, she was pleased with her progress, and quick to point out that her experiences in two worlds had helped her toward a number of important realizations. She had begun to see her bilingualism as a resource, and was fast overcoming her habitual shyness about speaking Spanish in public: whenever she overheard someone struggling to assemble fragments of broken English, she explained, "I see myself when I was a kid," and she was stepping in to help wherever she could. She had also acquired a certain easygoing openmindedness, an ability to consider diverse perspectives but ultimately chart her own course—this from growing up in a multiethnic, multilingual community, and from her struggle to come to terms with the assumptions and values of her extended family back in Mexico. Finally, her own experiences in school had convinced her of the value of bilingual education, a topic that she took up in her last essay of the semester:

> My opinion for bilingual education is that there should be programs funded by the government . . . How is a student going to be able to comprehend a second language, if the student has not had a strong foundation of his first language? By studying and understanding the basics such as grammar and structure, the student will be able to switch to another language.

Sylvia's argument was informed by knowledge of Cummins's (1979, 1981) "interdependence hypothesis," and by an abiding belief that she was living evidence of its truth. With her family's support, she had long struggled toward an "additive" bilingualism, toward a facility in two languages that would empower her in new ways without diminishing the importance of the old. Only as an insightful and ambitious young woman was she beginning to grasp the full complexity of that struggle, and to cast a discerning eye upon the lingering effects of what had happened to her— to her sense of linguistic competence, to her sense of identity—in second grade.

Adjustment to DPU

When asked if she were happy at DPU, Sylvia was decidedly upbeat: "I'm *very* happy here," she assured me; "I'm glad that I came, and for many reasons." Her father, she explained, had always wanted her to learn to be independent, and the experience of being away gave her a newfound confidence in her ability to get along on her own. While she admitted to fleeting moments of homesickness, Sylvia also boasted of her 2.9 G.P.A. and her ambition to "really push," to become a "better person," to fill in deficiencies in her academic preparation and build from existing strengths. If her glowing score on an initial placement exam was any indication, some of her greatest strengths were in mathematics, which she was "looking into" as a possible major. "Ever since I was a kid," she explained, "mathematics came easy to me—I get a thrill doing math." She could see herself going on for graduate work in math or engineering and possibly teaching at the college level.

Sylvia often spoke of the need for equity students to "get out of their cliques," noting that her upbringing in a multiethnic community had provided the sorts of experiences that were allowing her to thrive at DPU. Of Sylvia's closest friends on campus, two were Mexican and two African-American: "We can joke about race and not get offended," she emphasized, noting that she had learned much from their many discussions "about who we are and where we come from." Although her membership in M.E.Ch.A. initially opened a number of important doors, she had recently distanced herself somewhat from the organization. She was, however, continuing to serve as a DPU recruiter under the auspices of M.E.Ch.A.—leading campus tours and talking to local high school students "about what it's like to be away from home, in college." Sylvia spoke of this community service with particular pride, reporting that these highly positive experiences were helping to banish her lifelong fear of public speaking.

On the one hand, Sylvia felt a strong need to spend time with other Hispanic students—to speak Spanish ("music to my ears," as she described one recent conversation), and to reflect together upon the rewards and challenges of life at DPU; on the other hand, she worried that campus Anglos might regard her close association with the Hispanic community as a sort of protective cocooning, a shield that she insisted she neither wanted nor needed. Having grown up among people of many backgrounds, she was untroubled to find herself the only non-Anglo student in many of her classes. In a beginning-of-term interview, Sylvia flicked aside the many complaints she heard from others: "Sometimes if they feel that they're a minority," she speculated, "they feel real low or, like, low self-esteem. Who knows, you know? I'm a minority, I don't have a problem."

By the end of the semester, however, Sylvia's perception of ethnic relations at DPU had shifted somewhat. In an initial interview, she had insisted that she saw no signs of prejudice on campus, emphasizing that she refused to "look for trouble"; in a final interview, however, she noted that one of the most important lessons she had learned during her first year at DPU concerned the reality of discrimination. When an article in the county newspaper included the accusation that DPU equity students were recruiting for inner-city street gangs (see chapter 3), this young woman who liked to avoid "trouble" joined the protest march downtown. In the attitudes of security personnel and newspaper staff, Sylvia saw undeniable evidence of the same entrenched biases displayed in the article. This new awareness was, she admitted, initially shocking:

> I wasn't aware of what's out there when I was in high school. And then when I come here, it was a whole new world for me, you know, and I've never really been—well, I've been discriminated, but not to my face . . . and for me to actually see something like that, the first time it was really shocking to me. I thought, "damn," you know?

While Sylvia saw community attitudes as part and parcel of what she had observed on campus, she was especially disturbed to find DPU students—particularly students of color—discriminating against one another: "I thought we were all here to do something for ourselves," she mused, "not to put someone else down." Too many students, she observed, "see the outside first," missing the person within:

> I don't see the color. I mean, I can see the color, but I don't use it, like, "Oh, okay, she's white, she's this and this and this," or "She's black, she must be this and this and this," you know what I mean? I just look at them as the person.

Sylvia continued to regard racial prejudice as a hallmark of ignorance, of a failure to understand that human destinies are inextricably interwoven. Sobered by what she had observed during her year on campus, she was neither dejected nor sorry. While she had had to "cross many barriers," her ethnic identity was not associated in her mind with disempowerment or disadvantage. As far as she was concerned, her people were—like Sylvia the individual—up and coming:

> Like they say, "minorities." But I heard in the year 2000, that minorities are gonna be the majority, okay? Then why are we still being called "minorities"? Why can't we be called "underrepresented"? I like that better, you know, than "minority." I am not no minority. I am not in one of those little groups—I'm *underrepresented.*

Struggles with Writing

On the basis of her low score on an initial placement test, Sylvia had been assigned to a two-semester basic writing course. Impressed by her early work, course instructor Susan Williams gave Sylvia the option of moving into freshman composition after completing only the first semester—an offer Sylvia declined, electing to enroll in Williams's English 90 course. Although Williams saw Sylvia as the strongest writer in the second-semester class, she complained that Sylvia "doesn't go as much into depth as she needs to," and, lacking confidence in her writing ability, "sticks to real simple forms." Sylvia seemed well aware of these weaknesses, and spoke often of her desire to move beyond the five-paragraph essay, which she had first encountered in a writing workshop for Hispanic high school students; she also explained that while she had been influenced by her father's frequent reminders to "hurry up and get to the point," "writing teachers always want more detail."

When Williams asked for a written description of the "basic ingredients of an essay," Sylvia gamely recited the well-worn precepts she had heard again and again:

> The three basic ingredients of an essay are thesis, sufficient support for the thesis, and logical arrangement of that support. The thesis is the main point that the author wants to get across to the reader. Sometimes the thesis is mentioned somewhere in the essay or the reader has to determine what it is from the reading. Sufficient support for the thesis is giving backup evidence to the thesis. The support could be factual or not. Logical arrangement is how the author wants to arrange his thoughts. The arrangement makes the paper flow.

But as the semester drew to a close, Sylvia was still somewhat unsure of how to offer "sufficient support" or to make her papers "flow." Here, for instance, is a paragraph from a five-paragraph essay on "stereotypes" that she turned in during the final weeks:

> Society has stereotyped Latina women through the use of the media in television shows and movies. Sometimes the media shows Latinas as hookers that the white men prefer because they think that the women can give the men "good sex". Young Latinas have also been portrayed as being pregnant with two kids. The young women are also shown as having an abusive husband that beats her for the smallest reason, like a spot of dirt on the wall. Latinas are rarely cast

into the roles of college students or graduates. I am a Latina woman
who is in a four-year college, making something of my life. I don't
have an abusive husband or children, but I am still fighting these
stereotypes.

As with most of Sylvia's work, Williams felt that while this piece was
adequate, it seemed a bit lackluster, as if she had stopped short—short of
the livelier way with words that seemed well within her grasp, and short
of expressing the vital emotions that lay just beneath the surface.

When asked on a beginning-of-term questionnaire if she liked to write,
Sylvia had replied, "Not much. When I feel like writing, I write about
things that interest me." But even when writing about matters of profound
personal concern, Sylvia tended to rush, hurrying through the gist of a
story or argument rather than providing the sorts of detail that her writing
teachers always seemed to want. This tendency was evident in an essay
describing her mother's battle with cancer, which began with stage-
setting realism, but soon sped through long and significant stretches of
time:

> Seven years ago a major changed came into my mother's life and
> swept the family with her. One day I arrived at home after dance
> practice. I walked in the house, it was pitch dark, there were no lights
> on. Usually the stove light is on, but not this day. As I walked into
> the house, I got a strange feeling in my body. My mother was in her
> bedroom asleep. When she woke up, she looked as if she had seen
> a ghost. She was yellow, and her eyes were blood shot from crying.
> She did not want to tell me what was wrong. Eventually, she told me
> she had cancer. My mother said she had to make a decision whether
> to get an operation or not. She decided to go through with the
> operation. After the operation, my mother had to go through
> chemotherapy. The first day after chemotherapy, she came home all
> drained out. She felt as if her spirit was sucked out by a vacuum
> cleaner. I felt as if I also had cancer because I was defenseless to help
> or stop her suffering.

In an interview, Sylvia traced her struggles with writing to her troubled
linguistic background—to the fact that she had first learned to write in an
atmosphere of linguistic conflict and confusion, and at a time when she
was being prematurely immersed in an all-English classroom environment. Written words came forth more easily in English than in Spanish,
but somehow her composing still felt hidebound and unnatural; somehow
she had never come to visualize the reader over her shoulder, to see

composing as an opportunity to express or convey meanings. "I was always ashamed of my writing," she recalled. "My writing experiences are not as vivid as it might be to other people," she wrote in an in-class paper. "Ever since a kid, I did not like to write much. I would only write papers because they were assign to me." Only once, when a high school teacher had carefully led her step-by-step through a term paper assignment, had she felt both engaged and accomplished: "for the first time in a long time, I had confidence," she recalled. An ambitious paper which involved drawing upon secondary sources to compare three American writers, the assignment was more rigorous than anything Sylvia had yet been asked to do in college.

Describing Sylvia as a "very, very bright young woman," Williams remained puzzled by her acceptable but undazzling performance as a writer, surmising that Sylvia had developed "a little bit of a negative attitude about writing"; since "everything else comes pretty easily to her," Williams speculated, perhaps Sylvia was "a little upset that the writing doesn't." While Williams believed Sylvia had problems with "second language input," she held that "it's more in her case just a kind of a lack of interest in writing," since "her language interference problems aren't that severe." "I'd love to see something she's written in Spanish," she added hopefully.

Meanwhile, Sylvia's description of her enduringly troubled relationship with both English and Spanish belied the assumption that her writing was plagued by a clear-cut case of first-language "interference." Although Sylvia believed that her struggle to bring forth words in written English was rooted in the trauma of her early schooling, she only dropped hints to that effect in the presence of her teacher or group leader. Her written words remained mere kernels, the germs of ideas that might be encouraged to grow in the warm light of conversation and engaged feedback, but Sylvia was not particularly eager to move in that direction. When asked if her writing had improved over the semester, she replied, "not what I was looking forward to, or hoping. But that's only because of myself, because I brought it upon myself."

Group Leader's Response: Morgan

Morgan saw many similarities between herself and Sylvia—in their shared struggle against those who would accuse them of ethnic disloyalty, and in their propensity for stubborn resistance. While Sylvia's small-group attendance was about average for the class as a whole (she was present for twenty sessions and missed thirteen), Morgan considered her absenteeism excessive. Even when Sylvia was present, Morgan was often frustrated at Sylvia's level of participation—at her frequent reluctance to share writing and, occasionally, to participate in group discussions. One morning, as Morgan struggled to generate a brainstorming session, she paused to meet Sylvia's gaze: "You're giving me a bored look," Morgan observed; "You've got an intimidating look—I thought I was the only one with that look." At the last session of the semester, Morgan was a bit more direct: after Sylvia declined to read aloud the essay that she had been scanning silently, Morgan observed, "You're so feisty sometimes, I just want to, like, grab you by that hair." Unperturbed, Sylvia explained that she had a lot on her mind. "I'm teasin' you," Morgan quickly explained, if somewhat unconvincingly.

On those rare occasions when Sylvia brought in rough drafts of her essays, Morgan was an engaged and inquisitive reader, playing back her understandings of the text and encouraging Sylvia to extend her ideas. Late in the term, for instance, Sylvia handed Morgan a rough draft of an essay about her mother and asked her to read it silently. Sensing Sylvia's dissatisfaction with the piece, Morgan asked Sylvia what she felt was wrong. When Sylvia replied that it "wasn't balanced," Morgan worked to describe what she saw as the essay's controlling theme, and then asked a series of questions to help Sylvia clarify her purpose. Having agreed that the piece would contrast the mother's and daughter's differing aesthetic sensibilities, Morgan and Sylvia brainstormed details that would help bring alive these differences. Although they sometimes seemed to be lapsing into informal banter, Morgan periodically brought their conversation back to a focus, reminding Sylvia that the instances she was bringing up needed to illustrate a larger point: "What's the significance of that?" she asked repeatedly.

More often, however, Sylvia brought in only preliminary ideas, and they lapsed into mutually supportive discussions about life, often with no direct reference to writing. As she began to brainstorm an essay about stereotyping, for instance, Sylvia observed that many of her Latino friends back home "kind of feel jealous," openly criticizing her decision to go to a predominantly white college; "I'm doing something for myself and they're putting me down," she asserted. This struck a responsive chord in Morgan, who went on to describe her own struggle to overcome the conception that she was somehow "not black enough." The discussion continued in a later group, when Sylvia described how relatives back in

Mexico often assumed that she was leading an Anglicized existence of ease and wealth, and Morgan spoke at length of how estranged she would feel in the presence of African natives. Both displayed a sense of pride at the people they were becoming, at the paths they were pursuing, at their defiance of cultural conventions that both found rigidly prescriptive. One morning, when Sylvia was to speak to a group of Hispanic high school students, she noted that she "didn't care who was out there," that her goal was simply to communicate that she was happy to be pursuing an education. An appreciative Morgan literally cheered.

At other times, however, Morgan's strong identification with Sylvia interfered with her understanding of how their backgrounds diverged, and possibly impeded her efforts to help Sylvia formulate her own thoughts in writing. When Sylvia began brainstorming ideas for her essay about her mother's battle with cancer, for instance, Morgan mistakenly assumed that Sylvia's mother, like her own, had died of the disease: "My mom had cancer and died, too," she said, adding that when she tried to write about the experience for a timed essay exam, she had felt "too emotional" and found she "couldn't do it." "Oh, she didn't die!" Sylvia quickly explained, adding that while she might feel somewhat emotional about the subject, she was sure she could write about it. "Always be that critical writer," Morgan warned, "the objective writer . . . try to put yourself outside of the situation and look at it in terms of writing a story." In an interview, Sylvia explained that she found the cautionary note unnecessary; she, too, was a private person, she maintained, but before she could write on a subject, she had to feel personally connected to it.

In a final interview, Morgan observed that Sylvia seemed more receptive to her comments and a bit more open about bringing in her work. Still, Morgan shared Williams's feeling that although Sylvia had "complex ideas," she was readily frustrated by the effort it took to express them in writing:

> She tends to be a perfectionist. And so, when her writing isn't really, really good, uh, her writing is simple in a lot of ways, very simple. And it's, she doesn't like anybody to see it, you know, until it's really perfect. And then, I, I think that's her roadblock—she likes to do something, put it out and it's done, and it's nice and it's set out. And she looks nice all the time—her hair's always done nice, her makeup's always on, you know. And I think with her writing, she wants to do it once and here it is, it's nice and it's all done, and it's all wrapped up and it's tidy. It bothers her that, you know, she doesn't have it down the first time.

There's "something in her personality that comes out in her writing," Morgan observed—a tendency to "just present things," to forego "a deeper analysis." Morgan saw something of this same "black-and-white" approach in Sylvia's attitude toward the group:

> She doesn't worry about anybody else's trips, you know. We've had conversations before on tapes where she's like, oh, when we were talking one time about the students not showing up, she's like, "It doesn't bother me if they show up or not, I'm still gonna get ahead, I'm still gonna do my own thing," you know? So it's very clear: "These are my goals, these are what I'm doing, it doesn't bother me if anybody else does or not." She doesn't feel a need to bring the whole group along—if she's getting along, then that's fine.

Operating under the assumption that Sylvia was a native speaker of English, Morgan's analysis did not include attention to how Sylvia's linguistic background might play into her present difficulties with writing. What Morgan and Williams suspected was probably true to a point: embarrassed that her writing was not stronger, Sylvia was reluctant to share her preliminary efforts, and admittedly spent inadequate time revising her essays. An understanding of the psychological and linguistic reasons behind this behavior might have helped Morgan provide more consistently engaging and appropriate help; but such insight proved elusive, as Sylvia remained in Morgan's mind an intellectually gifted young woman whose problems with writing could be ascribed to a perfectionistic slant of character and, perhaps, a touch of basic laziness.

Perspective on the Adjunct Sessions

Sylvia began the semester with buoyant optimism, glad that Morgan was so much more personable than the critical, often-patronizing group leader that she had the previous semester. "I know I need help with my writing," Sylvia wrote in her journal after an early group session; "I feel this class is going to help because their is more of an individual help . . . the group leaders here are willing to help the students, if the students want help." The possibility that the adjunct sessions might foster peer response and discussion did not seem to occur to Sylvia, who described the small groups as a cost-effective but somewhat inefficient means of providing one-on-one assistance:

I think one-on-one you get more out of it. Because you can spend an hour and go through a lot . . . and with a group, a small group, you could only get to two or three people, and the other two or three are left. And they need, they might need more help, or less help, or whatever.

When asked about the effectiveness of group sessions, Sylvia's answers always focused upon her perceptions of her relationship with Morgan. In the beginning, Sylvia explained that especially since Morgan did not assign grades, she seemed less threatening and therefore more approachable than Williams: "I see her as a friend, but with the skills of a teacher," she explained, "and I'm not afraid of asking her, 'Morgan, what do you think of this?'" While Sylvia believed that she would ultimately have to overcome her writer's block on her own, she thought that her group leader could help by "having patience" and by understanding the source of her seeming resistance. It is important, she emphasized, that both teachers and group leaders "don't give up on the students— 'cause that's what I think a lot of teachers do, just give up on the student, and say, 'Well, they're not gonna do it, or they don't wanna do it.'"

In a final interview, Sylvia admitted that she had not attended the small groups as often as she had initially thought she would, explaining that she had gradually "lost interest." When I asked why, she began by assuming full responsibility ("I wasn't taking advantage of it, when I should have"), but she soon confessed her disappointment in Morgan's shifting attitude:

I don't know, I mean, I guess because the leaders lost the interest— not to all of us, but kind of lost the interest in working with some of us. And so, I mean, we're not that blind, if we see, if I see that Morgan's not that interested that day, you know, we'll just talk about things, you know. And I guess that's what happened.

Morgan's enthusiasm was "really off and on," Sylvia observed, noting particularly Morgan's tendency to get frustrated when the group seemed unresponsive: "Sometimes she would come to the group all pumped up and ready to go, and we wouldn't be all pumped up with her, but that's how reality goes." Although Sylvia felt that she understood Morgan's reaction to the group, she was still troubled by it:

I think she had high expectations of all of us in the beginning. But then when she got to know us, I guess through our writing and through our discussions, she, I don't think she had high expectations. I mean, I don't know—to me, when someone has high expectations and the person doesn't please them, or whatever, then the other person will be all, like, down and, like, "I didn't do my job right," or whatever.

Although Sylvia sometimes enjoyed the group's talks about issues and assigned readings, she generally preferred whole-class discussions, noting that they encompassed more perspectives. When it came time to share writing, however, Sylvia found even the small group a daunting audience:

> I'd rather have one person criticize me, and I know I can take that, than on a group basis. Because I remember in the beginning we would do, like, freewrites or whatever, and Morgan would want us to read them out loud, and I would, I would not like that. I mean, that sounds kind of strange, I mean, to, for me to say something like that, because I like to see myself as an outgoing person, that, "Hey, go ahead, read my stuff," you know. But I'm also that private person that I can only let one person read it at a time.

Sylvia traced the emergence of this fear to negative classroom experiences in elementary school:

> You know, because of the barrier of coming from a Spanish-speaking home to, going to a school and have English. Because I have the accent and stuff—but I didn't get laughed at, it's just that the teachers sometimes would say it in a nice way but I would take it as a negative way, you know. They would try to say it in a nicer way and I would get offended. That's just something I have.

Although Sylvia had initially looked to the small-group sessions as an opportunity to receive friendly, but expert, advice from a quasi-teacher, she eventually found that she preferred going to friends for assistance: "I get a lot of help on writing through my friends. I have friends that help me, and I always say, 'Here, check it for me, please' . . . And then when she would be finished, she'd go, 'Okay, what are you trying to say here?' and she'd help me that way." Sylvia had several friends whom she often approached for help: one who was enrolled in a basic writing class, another in freshman composition, and a third who was majoring in English. She explained that she felt more comfortable with them than with Morgan: "Because, well, because I know the kids, I know the students in my group, but I don't know Morgan that well . . . We've talked on a group basis and stuff about our experiences growing up and stuff, but I still don't have that personal touch."

On the other hand, when I played back taped segments of her work with Morgan, Sylvia seemed to realize that her feelings about the groups were somewhat more mixed than she had first allowed. Sylvia smiled, for instance, as she listened to the group brainstorm papers on stereotyping—a discussion dominated by herself and Morgan, both of them describing what it was like to be accused of "acting white." Morgan did most of the talking at first, but then Sylvia jumped in:

> I remember once, it was so funny to me, because I come from a middle-class background—although we're not white, we still come from the middle class and all. And this family, this guy, he's all, "You're white." I'm all, "No, I'm not" . . . Then he's all, "Why do you try to be, why do you try to act white?" And, well, I'm not, I know who I am and stuff, you know. It was when I was, like, in twelfth grade or something like that. And then he's all, that I was calling him a wetback and stuff, and I'm all, "No, I would never use that against my own race, I would never use it as a negative way. Joking around with friends I would."

Somewhat uncharacteristically, Sylvia had spoken at length in several instances on the tape, her words punctuated only by an occasional "Right" or "Uh huh" from Morgan. Sylvia seemed pleased to listen to her own words played back, but I was also interested in what she thought of Morgan's end of the conversation. Morgan had, after all, both begun and ended the discussion by talking about her own struggle against those who would call her "not black enough," and I asked Sylvia if she felt connected to this, if it helped her reflect upon her own situation. Sylvia responded:

> Well, I see it as kind of similar. We're going, like, we're in the same boat on that. Because when her friends tell her, "You don't act black," to me, what is "acting black"? Because you can dance, or you can sing, or whatever, you know? And when they tell me, "You're not Mexican," what is that? Just because I can't eat hot, spicy stuff, or I can't speak Spanish properly, or whatever? . . . I'm getting her input, and I'm getting her viewpoint. I mean, she has more experience than I do, and I can learn from her. You know, and how she has accepted it from society, and it hasn't brought her down.

When I asked if the conversation helped her gather ideas for the essay, Sylvia enthusiastically replied, "Yeah! . . . Because I did use some of the ideas that we talked about in my essay . . . it helped out, it really did."

Sylvia saw the session as typical of Morgan's teaching style: "Not formal, very informal—not very, but informal. Laid back, almost—she talks about her experiences all the time."

On the other hand, Sylvia found the next tape that I played back to be representative of something that she did not particularly like about Morgan's approach. The group was brainstorming descriptive essays, and although Sylvia volunteered only that she was thinking of writing about her mother, she was in fact mulling over memories of her mother's battle with cancer. Feisty and demanding, Morgan provided questions intended to nudge Sylvia toward greater specificity:

> *Morgan*: Um, okay, are you, like, thinking of any characteristics you wanna, like, throw out back and forth, that you want to talk about? How would you approach writing about this person?
>
> *Sylvia*: *[pause]* Uh, I don't know. *[laughs]*
>
> *Morgan*: You're a college student, you *should* know, that's why you're here . . . *[pause, then Sylvia starts to say something]* Any possible approaches?
>
> *Sylvia*: Just the way she has influenced me in my life.
>
> *Morgan*: What ways has she influenced you? Positive, negative? Let's start from there.
>
> *Sylvia*: Both.
>
> *Morgan*: Both?
>
> *Sylvia*: I mean, mostly positive.
>
> *Morgan*: Mostly positive?
>
> *Sylvia*: Yeah.
>
> *Morgan*: Influenced what about you?
>
> *Sylvia*: Um, well, like never to give up.
>
> *Morgan*: Okay, so if you put it under *[Sylvia starts to add something, but Morgan continues]*, if you put it under a broader, um, definition, what would you say, never to give up, never to, what would you call that, what she taught you, how she influenced you?
>
> *Sylvia*: What would I call it?
>
> *Morgan*: Yeah, what did she influence you, what did, what, what did she teach you? If you called it a whole body of things . . . *[pause]* So I guess what I'm driving at, what I'm trying to get to, is like values, morals, beliefs, ambitions.
>
> *Sylvia*: Oh, okay.

Morgan: You know? Okay. So while we're talking, why don't you, uh, make notes about things you could possibly approach about it, not saying that you have to. Let's start, you know, getting that together.

When asked for her response to the session, Sylvia filled in some of what was left unsaid in the rapid-fire exchange of questions and answers:

I did write an essay about my mother, about not giving up. And that to me was of value. I talked about her experience with cancer . . . *[softly]* and, um, how she had cancer twice, and she had just had, uh, my little sister. She had cancer the first time, it was about a year and a half after my sister was born, nearly two. And so, uh, I just saw how the . . . that was the first time, and the second time was about another year and a half, and that's when she got into chemotherapy and radiation and all that. And how the chemicals wore her down, and I would see her come home like a rag doll, almost. And how, one of my cousins was helping her into her bed, and stuff, that was in the beginning of the treatment. And how she had one of her breasts was taken out, and—I mean, just a lot of these things, like her body was taken, and it would bring her down physically, but not mentally. It would bring her up. She would look at us and cry and stuff, but then she would say, "No, I've gotta do it for them, I gotta keep on for them." I admire my mother a lot, I mean.

She said some of this in the paper that she wrote about her mother; why, I asked Sylvia, did she not talk about it in the small groups? She replied:

Because at the time Morgan asked me, and I wasn't ready for this, I wasn't ready for, to be asked all these kind of questions and stuff. And it was just that we were brainstorming, and I was just, that just popped into my head, afterwards . . . it wasn't personal because I talk about that experience a lot. And so . . . in the beginning, when she did have cancer, I would talk about it and I would cry. But I have gotten through that emotional phase. And I mean sometimes I do see her, and I go, "damn," you know, she went through all that, and I cry, but I won't let her see it. But, I don't know, it was okay.

Sylvia had been somewhat offended by Morgan's remark "You're a college student, you *should* know":

I didn't like that comment! I mean, just because you're a college student, and because you're here, doesn't mean you know every-thing. And it was something that she just threw me off on that one, like a curve ball there, you know. It didn't affect me, it's just that I know I'm a college student, and I know I don't know everything, but what I do know, I can say something about it, whatever.

Morgan approached the group in this insistent manner rather frequently, Sylvia observed. Sometimes, she admitted, the strategy was useful, especially when Morgan would ask questions that had not yet occurred to her—that way, Sylvia explained, "if someone else asks it . . . I can answer it . . . and that's more ideas for my paper."

Still, there was an apparent mismatch between the depth of Sylvia's emotions around this topic and Morgan's insistent approach in the session. When I played the same tape back for Morgan, she commented only that she was "starting to try and talk less," and that she was fairly happy with the response: "When Sylvia said, 'Oh, okay,'" Morgan observed, "it seemed like an 'aha' experience right there." But from Sylvia's point of view, Morgan had missed the mark, interpreting her initial reply of "I don't know" as an expression of insecurity or laziness rather than the plea for time that it in fact was. While Morgan's goals were to provide "collaborative" supports for student learning and to communicate high expectations, both were undermined by the assumptions that she had already made about Sylvia's level of motivation. Her intentions notwithstanding, these assumptions diminished Morgan's curiosity about what Sylvia was trying to say, and pulled at her efforts to provide tactful, appropriate guidance.

Part of being curious about students is to attend to the many ways in which they announce their need for privacy; Sylvia was, indeed, a private young woman, and it was important that Morgan not interpret her occasional guardedness as a personal rebuff or evidence of unresponsiveness. At the same time, however, Sylvia was extremely eager to talk about many aspects of her background, and noted again and again how much she enjoyed our conversations. Had Morgan only been encouraged to ask, I suspect that she, too, would have been provided some useful insights into the subtleties of Sylvia's background and current struggles with writing.

Endnotes

1.   Although Sylvia qualified as an EOP student on the basis of her parents' income, the family's real estate holdings rendered her ineligible for financial aid. Sylvia received academic counseling from DPU's EOP office, but she was the only focal student not receiving financial aid.

2. A study conducted by Lily Wong Fillmore (1991) suggests that such language loss and ensuing social disruption may be a quite common phenomenon among young children who are taught at school in a language other than that spoken at home.

6 Fannie

Cultural and Linguistic Background

At the first group meeting of the semester, Morgan asked Fannie about her reasons for attending college (see DiPardo 1992 for another look at Fannie). "I want to major in teaching," Fannie replied, "hopefully get a master's degree and teach." As a young child, Fannie had also dreamed of standing before a classroom: "God, when I was little, I used to play, you know, like, be teacher," she recalled, "that's what I used to do, me and my sister." Over time, Fannie's ambition would be informed less by eager imitation of her own teachers than by compassionate regard for young students. What Fannie did not say in the group that day was that she wanted to go to work at the same Navajo boarding schools that she had eventually grown to despise, that she longed to offer some of the intellectual, emotional, and linguistic support so sorely lacking in her own long years of schooling.

As a kindergartner, Fannie had been sent to schools so far from home that she could only visit her family on weekends. Navajo had been the only language spoken in her home, but at school all the teachers were Anglo, and only English was allowed. Fannie recalled that students were punished for speaking Navajo—adding with a wry smile that they had spoken it anyway, when the teachers were not around. The elementary school curriculum had emphasized domestic skills—cooking, sewing, and, especially, personal hygiene. "Boarding school taught me to be a housemaid," Fannie observed in one of her essays; "I was hardly taught how to read and write." All her literacy instruction was in English, and she never became literate in Navajo.

Estranged from her family and deeply unhappy at school, Fannie stayed for a time with an aunt and attended fifth grade in a nearby public

Portions of this chapter were originally published as "'Whispers of Coming and Going': Lessons from Fannie," *Writing Center Journal* 12:125-44. It is reprinted by permission of the publisher.

school. The experience there was much better, she recalled, but there soon followed a series of personal and educational disruptions as she moved among various relatives' homes and repeatedly switched schools. By the time she was sent away to a distant high school, Fannie was wondering if the many friends and family members who had dropped out had perhaps made the wiser choice. By her sophomore year, her grades had sunk "from As and Bs to Ds and Fs," and she was "hanging out with the wrong crowd," "smoking cigarettes and marijuana and drinking alcohol." By midyear, the school wrote her parents a letter indicating that she had stopped coming to class. When her family drove up to get her, it was generally assumed that Fannie's educational career was over.

Against all odds, Fannie finished high school after all. At her maternal grandmother's insistence, arrangements were made for Fannie to live with an aunt who had moved to a West Coast town where schools were said to be much stronger. Her aunt's community was almost entirely Anglo, however, and Fannie was initially self-conscious about her English: "I had an accent really bad," she recalled; "I just couldn't communicate." But gradually, she found that although she was homesick and sorely underprepared, she was holding her own. Eventually, lured by the efforts of affirmative action recruiters, she took the unexpected step of enrolling in the nearby university. "I never thought I would ever graduate from high school," Fannie wrote in one of her essays, but "I'm now on my second semester in college as a freshman." Her grandmother died before witnessing either event, but Fannie spoke often of how pleased she would have been. (Fannie took the name of this grandmother as her pseudonym in this report.)

Still struggling to find her way both academically and socially, Fannie bore the unmistakable scars of her troubled educational history. As she explained after listening to an audiotape of a small-group session, chief among these was an enduring reluctance to speak up in English, particularly in group settings:

> *Fannie*: When, when I'm talking . . . I'm shy. Because I always think I always say something not right, with my English, you know . . . *[pauses, then speaks very softly]* It's hard, though. Like with my friends, I do that, too. Because I'll be quiet—they'll say, "Fannie, you're quiet." Or if I meet someone, I, I don't do it, let them do it, I let that person do the talking.
>
> *A.D.*: Do you wish you were more talkative?

Fannie: I wish! Well I am, when I go home. But when I come here, you know, I always think, English is my second language and I don't know that much, you know.

A.D.:   So back home you're not a shy person?

Fannie: *[laughing uproariously]* No! *[continues laughing]*

I had a chance to glimpse Fannie's more audacious side later that spring, when she served as a campus tour guide to a group of students visiting from a Navajo high school in New Mexico. She was uncharacteristically feisty and vocal that week, a change strikingly evident on the audiotapes. Indeed, when I played back one of that week's sessions in a final interview, Fannie did not recognize her own voice: "Who's that talking?" she asked. But even as she recalled her temporary elation, she described as well her gradual sense of loss: "Sometimes I just feel so happy when someone's here, you know, I feel happy? I just get that way. And then . . . *[pauses, then speaks softly]* and then it just wears off. And then they're leaving—I think, oh, they're leaving, you know."

While Fannie described their week together as "a great experience," she was disturbed to find that even among themselves, the Navajo students spoke English:

> I realized that they're not speaking Navajo; every time I meet someone in Arizona, they'll be speaking Navajo, and these guys, they just speak English. I found out only, like, four of them spoke Navajo . . . That bothered me a lot, but then some, some might be lying though, because they're, like, embarrassed to speak Navajo, because back home, speaking Navajo fluently all the time, that's lower class. I used to think speaking Navajo was, like, like, really lower class, and I would speak English. Only at home I would, if my mom spoke to me in Navajo. And then when I was around my friends, I don't. But now *[laugh]* I speak Navajo all the time.

"If you don't know the language," Fannie wrote in one of her essays, "then you don't know who you are . . . It's your identity . . . the language is very important." In striking contrast to these students who refused to learn the tribal language, Fannie's grandparents had never learned to speak English: "they were really into their culture, and tradition, and all of that," she explained, "but now we're not that way anymore, hardly, and it's like we're losing it, you know." One day, Fannie hoped to attend a school on the reservation where she could learn to read and write in Navajo, and to pass that knowledge along to her students.

Fannie pointed to the high dropout rate among young Navajos as the primary reason for the reservation's enduring poverty, and spoke often of the need to encourage students not only to finish high school but also to go on to college. And yet, worried as she was about the growing loss of native language and tradition, Fannie also expressed concerns about the Anglicizing effects of schooling. Education is essential, she explained, but young Navajos must also understand its dangers: "I mean, like, sometimes if you get really educated, we don't really want that. Because then it, like, ruins your mind, and you use it to, like, betray your people, too . . . That's what's happening a lot now."

By her own example, Fannie hoped one day to show her students that it is possible to be both bilingual and bicultural, to benefit from exposure to mainstream ways without surrendering one's own identity: "If you know the white culture over here, and then you know your own culture, you can make a good living with that . . . when I go home, you know, I know Navajo, and I know English, too. They say you can get a good job with that."

Back home, Fannie's extended family was watching her progress with warm pride, happily anticipating the day when she would return to the reservation to teach. When Fannie returned for a visit over spring break, she was surprised to find that they had already built her a house. "They sure give me a lot of attention, that's for sure," she remarked with a smile. Many had not seen Fannie for some time, and they were struck by the change:

> Everybody still kind of picture me still, um, the girl from the past. The one who quit school—and they didn't think of me going to college at all. And they were surprised, they were really surprised. And they were, like, proud of me, too . . . 'cause none of their family is going to college.

One delighted aunt, however, was the mother of a son who was also attending a West Coast college: "She says,' I'm so happy! I can't wait to tell him, that you're going to college, too! You stick in there, Fannie, now don't goof!' I'm like, I'll try not to!"

On Easter Sunday, Fannie's extended family gathered at her cousin's house for a celebration of spring that combined Christian and Navajo traditions. After the requisite egg hunt, the family shared an "Easter cake": "They says Easter's, like, you know, everything's green, they're saying the earth's, like, being reborn, so they're saying happy birthday to the Mother Earth," Fannie explained. As it turned out, it would be a celebration of Fannie's regeneration as well. She was sitting beside her mother and sisters when her uncle called her name:

> He goes, "I want you to sit in front of these kids, I want you to sit right here, and sit in front of these kids, and tell them about school." I, I was surprised, but I didn't know, when I got up there, I didn't know what to say to those kids . . . I didn't know what to say! I was just, like, speechless! . . . Finally, I said, like, who I am, and then my plans and then what year I'm in college, and then I introduced my little sister and my mom, and my aunt. They all looked at her—and they're just sitting there, looking at me! And I'm like, "Don't look at me that way!" *[laughs]* I was picturing, too, at the same time, is this how I'm going to be when I start teaching, you know, kids will be looking at me? And then, and then I just told them about, after that, I just asked them what they would like to be when they grow up, you know, what they want to do. And some were, like, lawyers, you know, and I said, "Oh, that's good, that's a start," you know. And then, then I just talked to them about my school, and how school is . . . I said, "Don't give up."

Education, Fannie told them, provides a pathway out of their present poverty:

> I told them that they have so many scholarships, you know, there's scholarships, and I just told them to stay in school, that's what I told them. I said, "You don't want to end up like our parents. See, if you want to have, like, a nice house," I says, "do you guys ever dream of a nice house? You know, and driving a BMW and all that? You know, or at least nice, something very nice. Well, yeah. So if you really want it, go to college."

Adjustment to DPU

When asked what it was like to be an ethnic-minority student at a predominantly white campus, Fannie replied that "at first it used to bother me, but now it's not bothering me—I'm getting used to it." Having completed high school in the nearby community where her aunt and cousins lived, Fannie had already become somewhat accustomed to life away from the reservation. Still, she became terribly homesick from time to time—missing family, missing the stark beauty of the land, missing the familiar sound of spoken Navajo. Whenever she was alone, she talked to herself in her native language; and each night, as she sat in her dorm room trying to study, she would softly sing traditional Navajo songs.

More than once, Fannie almost dropped out of DPU: "Like, if I can't do my work, my homework," she explained, "I'll just get tired of it—I say this is too much for me. I don't mean it." More than once, she recalled, she phoned relatives back home to tell them "I don't belong here . . . this is not me, I'm just gonna quit, I'm just gonna go home, buy me a plane ticket." Her local aunt would invariably call her a "quitter" on such occasions, an accusation that never failed to elicit the desired response: "I'm not a quitter, I'm not quitting," Fannie insisted; still, she allowed, "sometimes you just get frustrated with school." Back at the reservation, newly supportive relatives took a slightly different tack: "If you mess up, they [the children on the reservation] see you mess up," her uncle told her. Observing Fannie's reluctance to return to school after a recent visit home, her mother said to her, "You know, you're stuck there [at DPU]. Go back and get your degree, and then come back and share with these kids." Fannie was glad that her family was finally becoming supportive of her educational goals: "my parents realize . . . how school is important, and they're proud of me," she explained. They had even begun encouraging children on the reservation to study harder at school, invoking Fannie as an example of someone who had managed to come back from the far side of defeat and discouragement.

Fannie believed that her ongoing struggle with motivation was shared by many other linguistic-minority students: "They just have, like, low self-esteem," she explained, "they all do, because, they think that learning English is, like really, it's hard, you know, and we give up easy, we do." Although Fannie longed for the company of other Navajos, she found the Native American Student Alliance and the campus Inter-Cultural Center to be strengthening influences. April had been proclaimed "Native Awareness Month" on campus, and Fannie spoke with uncharacteristic animation of her involvement in a number of the activities. One highlight was speaking to a counseling class about her grandmother; another was showing the visiting Navajo students around campus—five of whom, she was elated to hear, might be attending DPU the following year. Fannie smiled as she remembered one of them asking if she ever got lonely. She had answered yes, but then quickly explained that "'I have friends that are Indians . . .' I said, 'I just, like, call them or go be with them. And then you feel much better,' I says."

Although Fannie longed for the company of greater numbers of Native
Americans, she also welcomed her recent contact with students of varied
cultural backgrounds. Having grown up almost exclusively among Navajos, she confessed that she had held misconceptions about a number of
ethnic groups that her interactions at DPU were helping to reverse.
"Talking to them, communicating with them, socializing, all that," Fannie
explained, "I mean, I used to see them in stereotypes, but when you really
see the person, the person is different." More negatively, her first year at
DPU had also provided eye-opening insight into the intransigence of
racism: "God, it's sometimes, I just say why does that have to be there,"
she observed; "why can't everyone just be happy?" Although she particularly empathized with the frustration of DPU's Hispanic and African-
American students, she shrugged when asked what might help ease
tensions: "I don't think we can really change that stereotype thing," she
replied; "we can't really do anything about it."

Struggles with Writing

On the first day of class, instructor Susan Williams handed out a
questionnaire that probed students' self-perceptions of their strengths and
weaknesses as writers. In response to the question "What do you think is
good about your writing?" Fannie wrote, "I still don't know what is good
about my writing"; in response to "What do you think is bad about your
writing?" she responded, "Everything."

Fannie was arguably the most underprepared of the four focal students.
Shuttled from school to school throughout much of her childhood and
adolescence, Fannie described an educational odyssey both disrupted and
inadequate. Though taught to read and write English in the boarding
schools that she had attended as a young child, that instruction had been
neither respectful of her heritage nor sensitive to the kinds of literacy
challenges that she would face in the educational mainstream. She
explained in an interview that her first instruction in essay writing had
come at the eleventh hour, during her senior year of high school: "And my
teacher was just going over essays, essays, like, on *Hamlet* and all that,
and it was neat." Still, she explained, "I never got the technique, I guess,
of writing good essays, I always write bad essays." While she named her
"sentence structure, grammar, and punctuation" as significant weaknesses, she also added that "I have a lot to say, but I can't put it on paper

. . it's like I can't find the vocabulary." Fannie described this enduring block in an in-class essay she wrote during the first week of class:

> From my experience in writing essays were not the greatest. There were times my mind would be blank on thinking what I should write about.
>
> In high school, I learned how to write an essay during my senior year. I learned a lot from my teacher but there was still something missing about my essays. I knew I was still having problems with my essay organization.
>
> Now, I'm attending a university and having the same problems in writing essays. The university put me in English 30, which is for students who did not pass the English Placement Test. Of course, I did not pass it. Taking English 30 has helped me a lot on writing essays. There were times I had problems on what to write about.
>
> There was one essay I had problems in writing because I could not express my feelings on a paper. My topic was on Mixed Emotions. I knew how I felt in my mind but I could not find the words or expressing my emotions.
>
> Writing essays from my mind on to the paper is difficult for me. From this experience, I need to learn to write what I think on to a paper and expand my essays.

"Yes," Williams wrote in her comments, "even within this essay—which is good—you need to provide specific detail, not just general statements." Fannie noted in an interview that she panicked when asked to produce something within forty-five minutes: "I just write anything," she observed, "but your mind goes blank, too." Still, while this assignment may not have been the most appropriate way to assess the ability of a student like Fannie, both she and Williams felt it reflected her essential weakness: an inability to develop her ideas in adequate detail.

By the end of the semester, Williams continued to worry about Fannie's level of preparation; she had just barely passed the course, Williams confided, and would no doubt face a considerable struggle in freshman composition. Although Fannie also worried about the challenge of the next semester's course, she felt that she had made great strides in her basic writing class: "I improved a lot," she said in a final interview, "I think I did—I *know* I did. 'Cause now I can know what I'm trying to say, and in an afternoon, get down to that topic." Indeed, given opportunities to talk about her work and adequate time for revision, by the end of the semester Fannie's writing had become markedly stronger. Here, for instance, is an essay entitled "Home," written after a brainstorming session in her small group:

> The day is starting out a good day. The air smells fresh as if it just rained. The sky is full with clouds, forming to rain. From the triangle mountain, the land has such a great view. Below I see hills overlapping and I see six houses few feet from each other. One of them I live in. I can also see other houses miles apart.
>
> It is so peaceful and beautiful. I can hear birds perching and dogs barking echos from long distance. I can not tell from which direction. Towards north I see eight horses grazing and towards east I hear sheep crying for their young ones. There are so many things going on at the same time.
>
> It is beginning to get dark and breezy. It is about to rain. Small drops of rain are falling. It feels good, relieving the heat. The rain is increasing and thundering at the same time. Now I am soaked, I have the chills. The clouds is moving on and clearing the sky. It is close to late afternoon. The sun is shining and drying me off. The view of the land is more beautiful and looks greener. Like a refreshment.
>
> Across from the mountain I am sitting is a mountain but then a plateau that stretches with no ending. From the side looks like a mountain but it is a long plateau. There are stores and more houses on top of the plateau.
>
> My clothes are now dry and it is getting late. I hear my sister and my brother calling me that dinner is ready. It was beautiful day. I miss home.

"Good description," Williams wrote on this essay, "I can really 'see' this scene." But while Williams was fairly happy with the development of the piece, she was concerned about its style: "Try to use longer, more complex sentences," she added; "avoid short, choppy ones." In this and so many other instances, Fannie seemed unsure of how to make use of such advice, still too immersed in the challenge of committing thoughts to paper to think about fine-tuning their rhythms.

Fannie was obviously a student who needed lots of patient, insightful help if she were to overcome her lack of experience with writing and her formidable block. Only beginning to feel a bit more confident in writing about personal experience, she anticipated a struggle with the expository assignments that awaited her:

What Ms. Williams is doing . . . she's having us write from our experience. It'll be different if it's like, um, like in English 101, you know how the teacher tells you to write like this and that, and I find that one very hard, because I see my other friends' papers and it's hard. I don't know if I can handle that class.

Fannie was trying to forge a sense of connection to class assignments—she wrote, for instance, about her Native American heritage, her dream of becoming a teacher, and how her cultural background had shaped her concern for the environment. Still, as her teacher assessed Fannie's progress in an end-of-term evaluation, her wish that Fannie would say more in her essays assumed precedence: "needs to expand ideas w/examples/description/explanation," Williams had written, momentarily less concerned with questions of why, how, or to whom than with the lack of development so apparent in Fannie's papers. While Fannie's efforts to invest her writing with personal meaning were conceivably compatible with her teacher's goals, she would need lots of support to help flesh out her ideas with fluency and detail. The sheer number of support hours represented by the adjunct component struck Fannie as more generous than anything she had encountered before or would likely encounter again; but meanwhile, how best to make use of those hours was, as Morgan soon discovered, a question that defied easy answers.

Group Leader's Response: Morgan

As Morgan reflected back over her semester's work with Fannie, one memory emerged as uppermost: "I just remember her sitting there, and talking to her, and it's like, 'Well, I don't know, I don't know,' 'Well, what do you think about . . . ?' 'I don't know . . .'" Morgan longed for reassurance that she was providing some sort of help, but Fannie offered little by way of positive feedback: "Fannie just has so many doubts," Morgan observed, "and she's so, such a hesitant person, she's so withdrawn, and mellow, and quiet. You know, a lot of times, she'd just say, 'Well, I don't know what I'm supposed to write, I don't know'; 'Well, I don't like this, I don't like my writing.'"

Although Fannie seldom had much to say, her words were often rich in understated meaning. Early in the term, for instance, when Morgan asked why she was in college, Fannie answered hesitantly:

Fannie:	Well . . . *[long pause]* . . . it's hard . . .
Morgan:	You want to teach, like, preschool? Well, as a person who wants to teach, what do you want out of your students?
Fannie:	To get around in America you have to have education . . . *[unclear]*
Morgan:	And what about if a student chose not to be educated—would that be okay?
Fannie:	If that's what he wants . . .

At this point Morgan gave up and turned to the next student, unaware of the vital subtext—how Fannie's goal of becoming a teacher was enmeshed in her strong sense of connection to her people, how her belief that one needs an education "to get around" in the mainstream was tempered by insight into why some choose a different path. To understand Fannie's stance toward schooling, Morgan needed to grasp that Fannie felt both this commitment *and* this ambivalence, but clues to such understanding were neither abundantly offered nor readily received.

A few weeks into the semester, Morgan labored one morning to move Fannie past her block on a descriptive essay. Fannie said only that she was going to try to describe her grandmother, and Morgan began by asking a series of questions—about her grandmother's voice, her presence, her laugh, whatever might come to Fannie's mind. Morgan's questions were greeted by long silences, and she eventually admitted her frustration: "Are you learnin' anything from me?" she asked. Her voice sounded cordial and even a bit playful, but she was clearly concerned that Fannie did not seem to be meeting her halfway. In the weeks that followed, Morgan would repeatedly adjust her approach, continually searching for a way to break through, "to spark something," as she often put it.

The first change—to a tougher, more demanding stance—was apparent as the group brainstormed ideas for their next essays. Instead of waiting for Fannie to jump into the discussion, Morgan called upon her: "Okay, your turn in the hot seat," she announced. When Fannie noted that her essay would be about her home in Arizona, Morgan demanded to know "why it would be of possible interest to us." The ensuing exchange shed little light on the subject:

Fannie:	Because it's my home!
Morgan:	That's not good enough . . . that's telling me nothing.
Fannie:	I was raised there.

Morgan: What's so special about it?

Fannie: *[exasperated sigh]* I don't know what's so special about it . . .

Morgan: So why do you want to write about it, then?

Morgan's final question still unanswered, she eventually gave up and moved to another student. Again, a wealth of valuable information remained tacit: Morgan did not learn for several weeks that Fannie had grown up on a reservation, and Morgan understood nothing at all about Fannie's enduring bond with this other world. Perhaps caught off guard by Morgan's firm insistence, Fannie seemed to withdraw into an equally firm reluctance.

In the weeks that followed, Morgan's gathering sense of frustration became increasingly evident. One morning she tried to pull Fannie into a discussion about cheating on exams: asking Fannie what she thought, Morgan added rather sharply, "you hardly ever speak up." Rather than respond to the invitation to join the discussion, Fannie explained that she had been plagued by painful gallstone attacks during most of the semester, and had been vomiting so often that she had lost a great deal of weight. Flicking aside the earlier discussion, Morgan tried to reestablish connection with Fannie; after her mother died, she volunteered, she had thrown up a lot, too.

When Morgan took a few days off to attend the CCCC convention, she was admittedly perplexed about her work with Fannie. In our private conversations, she worried aloud that neither polite requests nor strong-arm tactics had persuaded Fannie to dive into the discussions, and that while informal chatter offered a sense of respite, it was not providing the needed help on writing. Then Morgan attended several convention sessions on collaborative learning, and suddenly felt infused with a clear new sense of direction: the answer, she concluded, was to take a decidedly nondirective approach, to ask open-ended questions, and to fill ensuing silences only with occasional paraphrases of what Fannie had already said. As she returned to DPU and her next encounter with Fannie, Morgan could hardly wait to try out the new strategy.

Only Fannie and one other student showed up for the first session after the CCCC convention, so Morgan had ample opportunity to experiment. Still struggling to produce an already past-due essay on "values," Fannie had only preliminary ideas, and nothing in writing. Morgan began by trying to nudge her toward a focus, repeatedly denying that she knew more than Fannie about how to approach the piece:

Morgan: What would you say your basic theme is? And sometimes if you keep that in mind, then you can always, you know, keep that as a focus for what you're writing. And the reason I say that is 'cause when you say, "well, living happily wasn't . . ."

Fannie: . . . *[pause]* Well, America was a beautiful country, well, but it isn't beautiful anymore.

Morgan: Um hum. Not as beautiful.

Fannie: So I should just say, America *was* a beautiful country?

Morgan: Yeah. But I dunno—what do you think your overall theme is, that you're saying?

Fannie: . . . *[long pause]* I'm really, I'm just talking about America.

Morgan: America? So America as . . . ?

Fannie: . . . *[pause]* Um . . .

Morgan: Land of free, uh, land of natural resources? As, um, a place where there's a conflict, I mean, there, if you can narrow that, "America." What is it specifically, and think about what you've written, in the rest. Know what I mean?

Fannie: . . . *[pause]* The riches of America, or the country? I don't know . . .

Morgan: I think you do. I'm not saying there's any right answer, but I, I'm—for me, the reason I'm saying this is I see this emerging as, you know . . . *[pause]* where you're really having a hard time with dealing with the exploitation that you see, of America, you know, you think that. And you're using two groups to really illustrate, specifically, how two different attitudes toward, um, the richness and beauty of America, two different, um, ways people have to approach this land. Does that, does this make any sense? Or am I just putting words in your mouth? I don't want to do that. I mean, that's what I see emerge in your paper. But I could be way off base.

Fannie: I think I know what you're trying to say. And I can kind of relate it at times to what I'm trying to say.

Morgan: You know, I mean, this is like the theme I'm picking up from your paper . . . *[pause]* I think, you know, you've got some real, you know, environmental issues here. I think you're a closet environmentalist here. Which are real true, know what I mean? . . . *[pause]* And when you talk about pollution, and waste, and, um, those types of things. So I mean, if you're looking at a theme of your paper, what could you pick out, of something of your underlying theme.

Fannie: . . . *[pause]* The resources, I guess?

Morgan: Well, I mean, I don't want you to say, I want you to say, don't say, "I guess"; is that what you're talkin' about?

Fannie: Yeah.

Morgan: Yeah. I mean, it's your paper.

Fannie: I know, I want to talk about the land . . .

Morgan: Okay. So you want to talk about the land, and the beauty of the land . . .

Fannie: Um hum.

Morgan: . . . and then, um, and then also your topic for your, um, to spark your paper . . . what values, and morals, right? That's where you based off to write about America, and the land, you know. Maybe you can write some of these things down, as we're talking, as focusing things, you know. So you want to talk about the land, and then it's, like, what do you want to say about the land?

What *did* Fannie "want to say about the land"? Whatever it was, one begins to wonder if it was perhaps lost in her group leader's unwitting appropriation of these meanings—this despite the fact that Morgan was taking such ostensible care simply to elicit and reflect Fannie's thoughts. While Fannie may well have been groping to say things for which there were no clear English equivalents, as Morgan worked to move her toward greater specificity, it became apparent that she was assuming the paper would express commonplace environmental concerns:

Fannie: I'll say, the country was, um . . . *[pause]* more like, I can't say perfect, I mean, was, the tree was green, you know, I mean, um, it was clean . . . *[long pause]* I can't find the words for it.

Morgan: In a natural state? Um, unpolluted, um, untouched, um, let me think, tryin' to get a . . .

Fannie: I mean everybody, I mean the Indians too, they didn't wear that, they only wore buffalo clothing, you know for their clothing, they didn't wear like . . . these, you know, cotton, and all that, they were so . . .

Morgan: Naturalistic.

Fannie: Yeah. "Naturalistic." I don't know if I'm gonna use that word.

Morgan: Well, maybe if you look up the word *natural* in your thesaurus?

Fannie: Yeah.

Morgan: . . . it'll maybe give you some words that'll start some other ideas for you.

Fannie: . . . *[pause]* I don't wanna use, I don't think I wanna use *beautiful.*

Morgan: Okay, look up *beautiful* in your thesaurus . . .

Fannie: I wanna say, I wanna give a picture of the way the land was, before, you know what I'm, what I'm tryin' to say?

The Navajos' connection to the land is legendary—a connection, many would maintain, that goes far beyond mainstream notions of what it means to be concerned about the environment. However, in her well-intentioned eagerness to understand and affirm Fannie's ideas, Morgan repeatedly used the term *environmentalism* to describe Fannie's stance. Later in this session, Morgan observed that Fannie was writing about concerns that worry lots of people—citing recent publicity about the greenhouse effect, the hole in the ozone layer, and the growing interest in recycling. She then brought the session to a close by paraphrasing what she saw as the meat of the discussion and asking, "Is that something that you were tryin' to say, too?" Fannie replied, "Probably. I mean, I can't find the words for it, but you're finding the words for me." Morgan's rejoinder was "I'm just sparkin', I'm just sparking what you already have there, what you're saying. I mean, I'm trying to tell you what I hear you saying."

Having said again and again that she wanted to avoid putting words in Fannie's mouth, Morgan laughed as she reviewed Fannie's final comment in an end-of-term interview: "I didn't want to find the words for her," Morgan mused; "I wanted to show her how she could find them for herself." Still, she admitted, the directive impulse had been hard to resist: "I wanted to just give her ideas," she observed, adding that although Fannie had some good things to say, "I wanted her to be able to articulate her ideas on a little higher level." Although it was obvious to Morgan that the ideas in Fannie's paper were of "deep-seated emotional concern," she also saw her as stuck in arid generalities: "'I don't know, it's just such a beautiful country,'" Morgan repeated sarcastically, "'and I don't know, well, oh yeah, I don't know.'" Although Morgan emphasized that she "didn't want to write the paper for her," she allowed that "it's difficult—it's really hard to want to take the bull by the horns and say, 'Don't you see it this way?'" On the one hand, Morgan noted that she had often asked Fannie what she was getting out of a session, "'cause sometimes I'll think

I'm getting through and I'm explaining something really good, and then they won't catch it"; on the other hand, Morgan emphasized again and again that she did not want to "give away" ideas that were properly her own.

Although Morgan sometimes did an almost heroic job of waiting out Fannie's lingering silences, she never really surrendered control; somehow, the message always came across that Morgan knew more than Fannie about the business at hand, and that if she were willing, she could simply turn over prepackaged understandings. While her frustration was certainly understandable, I often had the sense that Morgan was insufficiently curious about Fannie's ideas—insufficiently curious about how Fannie's understandings might have differed from her own, about how they had been shaped by Fannie's background and cultural orientation, or about what Morgan stood to learn from them.

Weary of Fannie's reticence, Morgan's efforts to probe its source likewise stopped short. When asked about Fannie's block, Morgan wrote it off to a cultural "problem": "You know, I would have to say it's cultural, I'd have to say it's her, you know, Native American background and growing up on a reservation . . . maybe . . . she's more sensitive to male-female roles, and the female role being quiet." On a number of occasions Morgan speculated that Navajo women are taught to be subservient, a perception that contrasted rather strikingly with Fannie's assertion that she was not at all shy or quiet back home. Hoping to challenge Morgan's accustomed view of Fannie as bashful and retiring, in a final interview I played back one of their sessions from the week that a group of Navajo students were visiting DPU. Fannie was uncharacteristically vocal and even aggressive that morning, talking in a loud voice, repeatedly seizing and holding the floor:

> *Fannie*: You know what my essay's on? Different environments. Um, I'm talking, I'm not gonna talk about my relationship between my brothers, it's so boring, so I'm just gonna talk about both being raised, like my youngest brother being raised on the reservation, and the other being raised over here, and they both have very different, um . . . *[Morgan starts to say something, but Fannie cuts her off and continues]* characteristics or something like that. You know, like their personalities, you know.
>
> *Morgan*: Um. That's good . . . *[Morgan starts to say something more, but Fannie cuts her off]*

Fannie: It's funny, I'm cutting, I was totally mean to my brother here
... *[Morgan laughs]* Because I called, I said that he's a wimp,
you know, and my brother, my little brother's being raised on
the reservation, is like, is like taught to be a man, he's brave and
all that.

Luis: *[another student joining in the discussion]* That's being a
man?!

Fannie: And . . .

Luis: That's not being a man, I don't find.

Fannie: *[her voice raised]* I'm sorry—but that's how I wrote, okay?!
That's your opinion, I mean, and it's . . .

Luis: I think a man is sensitive, caring, and lov- . . .

Fannie: *[cutting him off]* No, no . . .

Luis: . . . and able to express his feelings. I don't think that if you can
go kill someone, that makes you a man.

Fannie: I mean . . .

Luis: That's just my opinion . . . *[gets up and walks away for a
moment]*

Fannie: *[watching Luis as he wanders away]* Dickhead.

Morgan listened with a widening smile to the rest of this session,
obviously pleased with Fannie's sometimes combative manner and
unflagging insistence that attention be directed back to her. "Ha! Fannie's
so much more forceful," Morgan exclaimed. "And just more in control of
what she wants, and what she needs." When asked what she thought might
have accounted for this temporary change, Morgan sidestepped the
influence of the visiting students:

> I would love to think that I made her feel safe that way. And that I
> really showed her that she had, you know, by my interactions with
> her, that she really had every right to be strong-willed and forceful
> and have her opinions and, you know, say what she felt that she
> needed to say, and that she didn't have to be quiet, you know. I
> would, you know, people always tell me that I influence people that
> way. You know? *[laughs]* "You've been hanging around with
> Morgan too much!"

Hungry for feedback that she had influenced Fannie in a positive way,
Morgan grasped this possible evidence with a quite understandable sense
of relief. Fannie was not a student who offered many positive signals, and
it was perhaps essential to Morgan's professional self-esteem that she

find them wherever she could. In this move there was, however, a larger irony: if only Morgan had been encouraged to push yet a little farther in exploring possibilities, perhaps she would have found herself assisting more often in such moments of blossoming.

Perspective on the Adjunct Sessions

Although Fannie was ill for much of the semester, she attended the groups more regularly than most of the students, missing only six sessions. Embarrassed about her writing but also determined to improve it, she recognized the good intentions that informed Morgan's efforts and welcomed her help. No one had ever shown such interest in Fannie's work, virtually all of her writing instructors having failed to extend the extra support that she so needed. "In the small groups," Fannie explained, "I think I learned a lot from Morgan, but with Ms. Williams, she just gives us the assignment, and then she tells us what she wants us to do, and that's it . . . She says, 'If you need help, well, ask the group leader.'"

When Fannie said of Morgan that "she gets me pissed off," she wasn't complaining. Indeed, Fannie often felt that Morgan's "pushiness" was just what she needed:

> She, she, she, like, she pushes you, you know, she, she wants you to do it, and, and it's like she gets mad at you, but she doesn't get mad at you, but she has that thing that, it's like, "God, okay, I'll start writing" . . . it's funny, she'll say, "Is that all you're gonna write about, Arizona?" And I'll say no. She goes, "Describe it more." And I'll say, "It's peaceful" and all that, and she'll say, "Go on" . . . and then she gave me an example how she would write it.

"She can be bossy, yes, she can be bossy, she can be," Fannie observed, adding that "she just wants you to learn, I mean, that's what she's there for." Although Fannie saw her group leader as both friendly and knowledgeable, she became aware early on that Morgan demanded a focused effort:

> When we first met her I thought she was gonna be really nice, you know, cool, well, she is cool, I guess, but then when you really, like, writing essays, she really wants to get to that point, you know, she doesn't want to mess around, she wants to get to that point, writing the essay, she'll, you know, get to that. She can be a friend, then she can be like a teacher, too, at the same time.

Fannie felt that once she had decided upon a tentative focus for a piece, Morgan helped her see the need for detailed illustration and support:

> You know, you write something down general, like, she wants you to be more specific—like, point to it, she tells you that. And you like, "But that's it!" You know, but you say, "That's it." She's all, "No, Fannie," and you're like, "What is there to say anymore?" You know, and she's trying to tell you there's a lot more to say.

As we listened to an audiotape of one of their discussions, Fannie commented that "she's, um, giving me some ideas, maybe just what I want to say in my paper." When I asked if Morgan were putting words in her mouth, Fannie brushed aside the possibility that this might be a problem: "At times she will, but then when I think what I want to, what I'm trying to say, it mean the same thing, though . . . See, when she says this and that, then I have a lot of things to say about it, I have a lot of things to say in the paper."

Still, as Fannie listened to the tapes of their sessions, she allowed that "it's like she's speaking for me, [I'm] not [speaking] for myself, you know . . . it's real apparent, she did all the speaking, I didn't." Instead of considering the possibility that this imbalance may have been based in a shared dynamic, however, Fannie assumed full responsibility, noting how "stupid" she sounded on the tapes, "just saying, like, uh-huh, uh-huh, uh, yeah."

Fannie loved the lively play of ideas in the small groups, but when it came time to receive feedback on drafts of her papers, she much preferred one-on-one sessions with Morgan. Occasionally, Fannie recalled, Morgan would persuade her to share her work with the group: "Morgan will say, 'read it, read it,' you know, and she'll keep buggin' me, then I'll finally read it." On such occasions, Fannie would invariably go away regretting her momentary boldness:

> Well, I just feel awful when I read mine out loud, I just don't like it. But I usually set up an appointment with Morgan . . . but I don't like to read my rough drafts out loud . . . I just don't think my writing's that great, I mean, I don't want them to know, you know, that "she writes terrible, that she's not the greatest writer," or something . . . I just, I just can't read it . . . They'll say, "That's good, that's good," you know . . . They help you, but then when they help you I feel awful again, because I want [it to be] my own.

Fannie would probably represent an instructional challenge to even the most seasoned instructor, and to this relatively new adjunct, she seemed to evoke more frustration than satisfaction. Looking closely at Morgan's work with Fannie, one readily detects missed opportunities, imperfect connections, blind spots; but it is worth noting that to Fannie, none of this canceled the fact that Morgan was the first person ever to show an abiding interest in her writing. "She wants you to learn, you know, like, how to write," Fannie explained, "that's what she's there for." Comparing herself to the many equity students who "know what they want to write about," but "then they tell themselves they can't," Fannie voiced appreciation for Morgan's help:

> And it has to do with being a minority, too . . . they probably put themselves, just because they're a minority they can't do this or that. I think it's low self-esteem . . . They have something inside, but they can't bring it out. And I tell my group leader, you know, how I feel and all that, I mean, you can tell your group leader how you feel, you know, about writing, you know, and I think all the students do that. They can tell their group leaders how they feel and how they think about their writing. And that's what they need, too, instead of just having all that build up inside.

While Morgan continued to see Fannie as mostly closed and reluctant, Fannie described herself as opening up, as talking with Morgan about that "something inside . . . about writing." In the quiet evidence of this movement rested some promising instructional clues as well, signaling the need not only to "talk less," but also to listen more.

7 Al

Cultural and Linguistic Background

In one of his essays, Al described his home community, Southwood, as "a playground of death and poverty," a place where "you could step on a person's shoe and be shot for it," where "money and revenge were the operative words."[1] He described how he had been shunned by many of his old friends for his decision to pursue an education, for working long hours after school at minimum wage while they amassed small fortunes dealing drugs. Still, he hoped to go back after graduating from college, to establish a career there, and to "help out." As he explained in an initial interview, his main goals were to ease his mother's situation and become a positive force for community change:

> My main goal in why I'm going to college is so my education can be better than what my father or mother had, you know, and so I can go back to them, you know, when I'm finished, and well-established, go back to them, because I feel I owe my mother a lot. I feel I want to go back and help her get out of most situations that some mothers are in, like always worrying about different things, like bills or something like that. I want to go back and help my mother out of that situation. God willing, if I can get established, well enough to take care of my mother and myself, that's what I want to do. And also, I want to go back into my community, you know, because no one seems like they cares about the generations that's coming up. And I want to go back and do different things to try to get them out of the gang situations, the drug situations. That's my main goal, to help people—I like helping people.

But to move closer to these goals, Al found himself at a distant college, trying to speak and write a still-alien variety of the language. Although determined to adopt mainstream English while on campus, he was still struggling with his new dialect on many levels; "I feel [more] comfortable," he explained, "talkin' the way, you know, I was brought up to talk" (see Labov 1972). He noted that because he still thought in Black English, each time he spoke up in class he had to pause to translate his thoughts into mainstream utterances. Sometimes, he acknowledged, this presented a cognitive overload:

> If you listen to me you can kind of get some sense of how I talk, you know, you can get some sense of how I try to say things, but it comes out a different way. One thing's going through my mind, but it just comes out of my mouth, not differently, but not in the sense I was thinking about it.

When I asked if he still spoke Black English to friends and family back home, Al at first said no, but then hastily changed his answer:

> No, not really, I just speak in dialect with, uh . . . *[pause]* well, yes, you can say yes I do. At times, you know, back at home, when you leave a certain way, people expect you to come back the same. And if I go back talking like I'm, you know, this much higher than they are, they wouldn't respect me, you know. It's like they would respect me but they wouldn't get as close to me as they would usually do because they're thinking, "Oh, he think he's too good for us, he talkin' this kinda language." And all this and that . . . And when I go back, I talk, you know, the way I used to talk, you know, back then, but I don't feel I would like to change, for anyone. And my friends are always going to be there for me, so I don't feel I'd like to do anything to jeopardize my friendship.

When asked what would happen if he began speaking at home the way he was speaking at college, he replied, "I'd stay in the house, with my mother . . . I wouldn't go out with the same friends I hung with . . . That's the main thing about going home, you know . . . they go, 'Well, you think that because you're in college you can't . . . hang with us' . . . that's the sort of thing I'm afraid of."

Al's home community was entirely African-American, and although it was nestled within a city noted for its cultural diversity, he was a teenager by the time he first engaged in conversation with an Anglo. Although he felt tremendous community loyalty, he had become somewhat secretive about his roots since coming to DPU. Aside from private conversations with his African-American roommate, he was trying to adhere as unswervingly as possible to mainstream English:

> My roommate, you know . . . I'll speak with him, uh, and my buddy that, that was here last semester. But he went in jail, up here. I would

speak in dialect with him. I try to get my being from Southwood
away from up here, I don't really like people knowing where I grew
up at. It's not like I go around parading it around campus . . . Some
people don't even know where I'm from.

The first member of his family to attend college, Al was charting new
ground, undergoing a process of linguistic and cultural change that was
realigning his loyalties and leading him toward a promising, but still
uncertain, future. Only when he visited home would Al realize just how
much he was changing:

Every time I go back, my mother always say, "Well, you've
changed here and you've changed there." And I feel better, you
know, 'cause I'm like, why not change, you know, change for the
better at least, you know, so. She tells me every time I go home. I
haven't been home in a long time, so I don't know how much I've
changed.

Adjustment to DPU

At the beginning of his second semester at DPU, Al was still struggling
somewhat unsuccessfully to achieve a sense of membership in the
campus community. Even during his first day in the Summer Bridge
program, he had felt that other students were eyeing him with suspicion:

The first day that I came in, I felt as if people were looking at me,
and staring at me, for the way—I, I don't even know why, it seemed
as if, you know, as if my appearance, like something was *on* me, you
know, something, like, I smelled bad, or, you know, they looked at
me crazy . . . It seemed like I, I don't even know, it's just like people
stared at me constantly before they even knew me, you know . . .
after the meeting, someone came up to me that I didn't know, and
they came up to me and asked me which gang, you know, how long
. . . they asked me where I was from. And when I told them, then,
you know, they looked at me crazy, you know. I guess they just
knew I was from Southwood and I was supposed to have been in a
gang or something. And that they were tempted to be afraid of me
because of what I might do, or they didn't trust me with anything,
like any of their possessions, or anything like that, there was a look
on their face like that. And from that point on, you know, me being
away, you know, I never been away from, from Southwood before,
I been to Alabama, but that's not, that's not, I was just there with

family. I never been away to get stereotyped in that manner, that quickly. Like in Southwood, you know, people never stereotype me as being a gangster . . . I didn't dress like a hardcore gangster would, you know. I was always . . . someone who made it through without having to join a gang.

Al was only beginning to overcome this negative stereotyping when, during the second month of the academic year, his best friend was arrested for date rape[2]:

What really exposed the whole situation was when my buddy went to jail for something that happened in the dorms. After that, people looked at me differently again, even people that I knew looked at me differently. I had . . . I had everything established, where people stopped thinking of me as a regular old hootin' from Southwood, until that situation happened there. And then they thought again . . . he's from Southwood, so this is always gonna be in there, so you can't trust him. I got this sense, a feeling towards people again, there was nothing I can do. So I just stopped caring, you know, I just stopped speaking to some people. And there's nowhere that it's, like, you know, that it hurting me, you know, 'cause I'm not used to talking to people, you know, about myself anyway, you know. Everyone minds their own business, so I just started minding my own and, and not worrying about how people felt about this way or about, you know, what I came up here to do.

Although Al described himself as a relaxed, "kick-back" sort of person who could "get along with everyone fine" and be "sociable with all races," his growing sense of alienation was clearly taking a toll. When I asked if he had anyone he could talk to about all that had happened, he bowed his head, wiping away tears. "I'm just holding my own end," he said finally, "'cause I don't want anyone else worrying about me, and worrying about what I'm going through."

Al explained that he had memorized the positive-thinking poem "The Man Who Thinks He Can," and that he often repeated it to himself in moments of doubt. "If you think you can do something," he said, brightening a bit, "then you can do it." He allowed that few people recognized his idealism or depth—his drive to help pay his own school expenses, his desire to help mend his torn community, or his abiding sorrow over the realities of ethnic discrimination. Nor did people recognize Al's hidden intensity, the tension between his fierce independence and equally fierce desire to belong:

> I never really give too many people the chance to really see me—
> I never really give people a chance. I always, I've never gotten
> serious with too many people up here at Dover Park, but the people
> that I get serious with understand where I'm coming from, and
> what's my motivation.

At the end of the semester, Al joined an African-American fraternity, finally finding some of the social acceptance he had so sorely needed all year. Gone, however, was his early commitment to cultivating friends of all races; gone, too, was much of his vulnerable sensitivity, his penchant for sad reflection upon inequity and prejudice. He was distant and careful in a final interview, avoiding eye contact and declining to talk about campus controversies. He expressed happiness, however, about being accepted into his fraternity, and about the personal, academic, and professional assistance his new network would provide. When a fellow fraternity member passed by, Al broke into a broad grin and flashed the group's hand signal, his momentary exuberance in striking contrast to his new reluctance to talk with me.

As he emerged from the depths of his early struggle, Al began to speak of his adjustment to DPU with greater detachment. Being one of the only African Americans on campus was, he readily admitted, "*very* rough," especially "coming from a neighborhood . . . where you're not used to seeing so many, you know, Caucasian people." When he finally made the decision to stay, a prime factor was the support that other African-American students had begun to offer: "they're my best friends," he explained, "they'll stick with you, you know." While he remained cordial to campus whites, he had come to accept that they "wouldn't understand" his background or current struggles. Al pulled back into a tightly knit community of students who *would* understand; and if he remained something of an idealist, he was no longer naively hopeful, his openness and vulnerability tempered by an exceptionally trying freshman year.

Struggles with Writing

In an end-of-term evaluation, course instructor Susan Williams noted the unevenness that she had observed in the quality of Al's written work: "When you're on, you're on," she wrote, "but when you're not . . ." While she praised his "excellent ideas," Williams noted a certain inconsistency in his "attitude" and level of "effort." Al had also taken Williams's first-semester basic writing course, and he often noted that he "liked her style of teaching" and felt that his writing was improving. He agreed, however, that his motivation tended to fluctuate—an inconsistency he traced to his ongoing struggle to move beyond the personal experience essay:

> I like to write, to the extent that I like to write about things that I like, you know. It's hard for me to write about things that I'm not real interested in. I'll do it, but I don't feel it's the best writing I can do. Like on my last essay, when she [Williams] told me that it was the best writing that she's seen me writing, I was writing about my feelings. My feelings are all at home—my neighborhood. People might put it down, but I love it. And that's when I write the best.

The essay to which Al was referring described his rather complex bond with Southwood. He worked longer on this piece than on any other he had written all year, poring over his thesaurus in search of the perfect word, the apt phrase to capture the striking contrasts among his many images of home. Here are the first two paragraphs of that essay, entitled "Living Day to Day in Southwood":

> Drug dealers, pimps, thugs and thieves: those were the categories people generally placed me in whenever I mentioned to someone that I was from Southwood. No matter how well I presented myself, I was always thrown into a pot of stereotypes and misconceptions that stuck to me like the odor of a garbage dump. Southwood however, meant much more to me than the average outsider could see.
>
> For me, Southwood meant struggle and survival of the fittest for who ever lived there. During my childhood years, Southwood was a great place to live and grow up. It was no different than any other community: we all had our problems and each of us dealt with them accordingly. As a child, I frolicked endlessly in my neighborhood park at the top of the hill. I remember being able to go by myself to the park, hop on the swing and ride it until I could almost fall backwards with laughter and joy. I recall rolling, flipping, running and jumping through the grassy jungle of Howell Park, which was my home away from home while playing. During this time in my life there was an air of happiness, community pride and love in Southwood that could not go unnoticed by any outsider visiting Southwood for the first time.

On a beginning-of-term questionnaire, Al explained that he was learning to enjoy writing more than ever before, noting that it provided a vehicle for "expressing feelings." In an interview, he observed that "anything that's personal to me, I can write about"; on the other hand, he admitted, "if you're not interested, you just do the minimum, to get over." In "Living Day to Day in Southwood," Al approached a personal topic with unprecedented fluency and, occasionally, artful style. Here, on the other hand, are the first paragraphs of an essay that Al wrote soon afterward on the subject of "justice," this in response to an "argumentative" assignment:

> In my opinion, justice is the single most influential force controlling our lives today. In the following pages I will cite reasons exactly why justice has the overpowering effect on us it does. During your reading you will find exactly how the definition of justice has gone astray.
>
> Since the beginning of time, we have had a legal system of one sort or another. One of the earliest legal systems was that of egytptian rulers. Their reign was supreme. For example, King Tutankhamen ruled egypt for over eleven years. Was there no corruption? None! It was absolutely impossible. Pharoahs ruled with iron fists and crushing amounts of non-existant. During this time there was no real sense of justice: the only law was that of the pharoahs. From this we can determine that once justice is divided, many factors come into play; one of these such factors being corruption.
>
> Through the years we have evolved into a complex animal, capable of establishing laws supposedly for and by the people. Which brings us to present day America so great. In egyptian time there was a great deal of control v.s. today where on a common day you might find fifty killings in a state, under the table bribes, insider trading scandals, mass murderers going scott free or finding freedom in the form of a technicaity. Is this justice? Yes, for the rich, the murders or the well connected.

Although Williams noted that Al had "good ideas here," she also commented that "I sometimes felt a bit lost in this essay." The latter perhaps seems the more candid observation, as this piece meandered from focus to focus, bereft of connecting threads. As Al admitted, when writing about "things that are not really personal," he would sometimes "just like . . . write anything, just rhetoric, you know."

It was as though writing were two different activities for Al: the engaged process of describing matters close to the heart, of carefully translating his thoughts into the language of the academy, and the slapdash recording of half-cooked ideas, committed to paper for the sole purpose of fulfilling a requirement. He enjoyed sharing writing that he had struggled long to produce, but he kept his lesser efforts hidden from view:

> If I put, you know, quality time into my writing, I know it's a good essay, I've rewritten it three and four times, you know, then . . . that's no problem . . . but I'm just saying just, like, just essays that I just write, some of 'em I don't feel confident enough read out in front of, you know, to anybody . . . Sort of like rough drafts—you want it to be real good before you share it with a lot of people . . . Because I, myself, I don't like, I never like to look bad, so, like, if I have like an essay that's not, not well written, you know, there are a lot of mistakes, you know, I can't deal with that.

Proud, private, and self-reliant, Al was loath to expose his fledgling first thoughts, his conception of the composing process having more to do with rugged individualism than the purported benefits of collaboration. While Al increasingly found himself in the company of friends who were more than willing to talk with him about his work, he explained that "most of the time I'm very independent . . . I never liked asking people for anything."

Group Leaders' Response

Morgan

Williams first assigned Al to Morgan's group, this in the hope that he would find her charisma and enthusiasm irresistible—that he would attend regularly, as Williams later said with a wry smile, "just for the chance to sit next to her." Likewise regarding Morgan as a natural role model for other African Americans, the Dean of Academic Programs had also appointed her Al's equity-student mentor, charged with helping him over the academic and social hurdles of his freshman year. The match had seemed both logical and fortunate: while Al was just beginning his college career, Morgan was already a campus success story, and, as a fellow African American, was in an apparently ideal position to provide appropriate support.

Many were surprised, then, when an embittered Al asked to be moved out of Morgan's group during the second month of the semester. She was puzzled and hurt by his sudden disgruntlement, which he explained only in sketchy terms to Williams and not at all to Morgan. Only in retrospect do the early signs of developing trouble become apparent—in Morgan's reflections upon her initial work with Al and in their superficially cordial conversations in the group. In a beginning-of-term interview, for instance, Morgan seemed keenly aware that Al had grown up in a community where gang violence was endemic, and implied that his background and current coterie of African-American friends were holding him back:

> I get the feeling sometimes, you know, I think he's seen a lot. One time we talked about how he'd been down in Southwood, and he'd seen a cousin of his, they were in a car and there were some kind of gang things going on, and he'd been down there for the weekend, and he said his cousin got out of his car and went back and there was another car, and just shot this guy point blank . . . It was just some kinda shocking to him. So with Al, sometimes I feel he's just caught between two worlds, and, um, I see he's got quite a following of friends and stuff on campus. One time we walked into the pub, and he was supposed to be in there with us, and we happened to walk in there, he was in there hanging out and eating and stuff, and I'm like, "Okay Al, come on, you know, let's go". . . I think he's fine with his writing, he hasn't shown me anything, he hasn't shown up a lot . . . I'd like to see him, you know, give himself more of a chance, you know, and take his schooling more seriously.

Morgan went on to explain that as a fellow African American, she felt that she was in a particularly good position to help convince Al of the value of academic success:

> I think I'm kind of being a little manipulative, but I'm trying to pull in the whole race and ethnicity thing, and, well, I'm black too, and I'm a minority too, you know, I haven't succumbed to any, which I think a whole lot of minority people tend to do, oh well, you know, "don't be an Oreo," you know, and "don't be black on the outside and white on the inside." They think you're selling out. And I'm trying to use this to say, "Well, I'm not selling out . . . I'm trying to get this feeling across, that I'm not any different from you, at all, except that I'm choosing to be real involved in my education."

There's a subtle afterburn to that last statement, with its implication that Al was somehow not choosing to be "real involved" in his education, his background having put him at some sort of disadvantage. Around this same time, Morgan made a similar statement in a group session: Al had been talking about how the students in his high school had given the teachers a "hard time," and Morgan responded by noting that "I grew up in Dover County, where most of the parents cared about their kids, and there were organized sports and stuff." Morgan made this remark in a friendly manner, seemingly unaware that she might be communicating the assumption that Al's family had not demonstrated similar regard for his welfare.

Although Morgan noted that she tried at all times to be "real respectful," she was drawn to the challenge of penetrating Al's occasional silences. Sometimes, she explained in an initial interview, she would approach him as a "really big mommy," expressing concern when he seemed downhearted and inviting him to talk about his troubles. When Al politely declined such overtures, Morgan tried other ways to establish rapport. Although she said in an interview that she had never minded living in a predominantly white community, Morgan joked with Al about the demographics of Dover Park: "Ow, *white*, you know?" When he came in late to an early group session, Morgan yelled to him from across the crowded room ("Hey, buddy, over here"), and she gently reminded him of looming deadlines. Always, Morgan worked to communicate a sense of solidarity, stressing that he could use the group time "to get part of your requirement out of the way, since we need to be here anyway, right?" When Al came to the group unprepared with preliminary ideas or rough drafts, she brushed aside his excuses, insisting that his writing was promising and deserved his concentrated attention; "we've gotta get you started on something," she remarked during an early discussion. Meanwhile, Al sidestepped Morgan's questions about his work, preferring to sort through his initial ideas on his own, respectfully declining her invitations to explore his options collaboratively.

When Al went to Williams to request a transfer out of Morgan's group, he primarily complained of her tendency to act "like his mother," pointing with particular emphasis to a recent occasion when she had criticized his eating habits. Williams summarized the conversation for both Morgan and Kalie, and among the small-group leaders, the quasi-Freudian phrase "Al's problem with his mother" soon became shorthand for the prevalent interpretation. Hearsay became accepted truth, and a perhaps more important aspect of their rift was overlooked and forgotten.

In their final sessions together, a gathering conflict over cultural and linguistic difference was plainly evident, particularly as the group discussed an assigned essay on Black English. Entitled "What's Wrong with

Black English," the piece was written by an African American who took heated exception with those who see vitality in the black vernacular. "It hurts me," the author wrote, "to sit in lecture halls and hear fellow black students complain that the professor 'be tripping dem out using big words dey can't understand,'" and it hurts even more to be "stripped of my own blackness simply because I know my way around the English language . . . I don't think I talk white," she concluded; "I think I talk right."[3]

A few days before Al decided to leave Morgan's group, they read this piece aloud together, each student taking a paragraph. Urging the students to move in closer so they could all hear, Morgan turned to Al and remarked lightly, "Come on, I won't bite." The same could not be said of the ensuing discussion, in which Al struggled somewhat futilely to articulate his point of view while guarding his own linguistic background. Morgan began the discussion by stating her own belief in the importance of knowing mainstream English, and although Al did not disagree—indeed, he repeatedly referred to standard English as "correct English"—he was eager to explain that his relatives had not consciously chosen their variety of the language:

> *Al:*   . . . you know, the parents, like, say our parents or my grandparents, were not really taught the correct English, really, let it go, now, I don't know how to, I don't know how, uh, they come up with this, you know, 'bout how I feel bad for, you know, kids that come up talking Black English. They weren't taught . . . their parents weren't taught any other English . . .

> *Morgan:* Okay, but I think one of the points she's making . . . she feels it hurts her to hear children, who are young black children, who by virtue of the fact of their blackness, and the culture and society that we live in, are gonna be disadvantaged against already, but I think she said it hurts her to hear them talk Black English, knowing that maybe that's all they're gonna learn, I mean, the way I look at it . . . *[Al starts to say something, but Morgan overrules, keeps going]* The way I look at it, the way I look at it—let me, I'm sorry *[addresses this to Al, then laughs]*—I look at Black English, like another language, like you can look at Spanish, or you can look at French, or you can look at anything. But when people come to the United States, they need to learn standard English, because that's, that's what's gonna to make you marketable. I mean, you may not agree with all that culture . . .

Al: But you have to think of it like this, too . . . *[Morgan tries to say
             something, but Al overrules, keeps going]* Racism is still going
             on. And, um, um, by them learning the English that they're
             learning, is that their parents are not really aware of what's
             going on, what they're saying right now, because they weren't
             taught the correct English from the beginning. I know my
             mother, she didn't even finish her high school, um, you know,
             whatever, she didn't finish high school. Um, and I brought up,
             I was brought up like I am now, you know, I was . . . maybe
             through generations to come, then, you know, all black people,
             they'll grow up learning the correct English. But now, they have
             to get taught in school.

Keenly aware of the stigma so readily attached to his people and their
language, Al leapt somewhat awkwardly to defend his family's use of
Black English—a variety they couldn't help but speak, never having been
taught "the correct English." Difference—his difference—had been cast
as deficit, and he scrambled to respond. Only a few moments later, when
Morgan spoke of how she switched "dialects" across various settings, did
Al seem moved to anger, suddenly aware that she did not truly appreciate
what it meant to be bidialectal:

Morgan: *[quickly, animated]* When I'm . . . hanging out with people with
             whom I work . . . my, uh, speech, uh, and my dialect is
             completely different, and then when I'm here in school . . .

Al: *[trying to interrupt]* It depends on . . .

Morgan: . . . my dialect is *completely* different . . .

Al: I'm sorry, but it depends on who you grew up around.

Morgan: That's true, but I mean, you grow up around a system of people,
             and a system of behaviors, that are just inherent to the group,
             and that language and, um, slang terms . . .

Al: The more black people you grew up with, the more Black
             English you're gonna come up with.

Morgan: That's exactly it; see, I didn't grow up with a lot of black people,
             so I don't have the control of a lot of Black English . . .

Morgan concluded the discussion by noting her resentment when people
charge that her use of mainstream English renders her somehow "less
black." When the group met again, she made a similar speech: "just how
we said that the other day," she began, "like how in the hell can anybody
tell me that I am not black, or that I do not act black. What does acting

black mean? You know what I mean?" Al, who had not said anything all hour, suddenly spoke up: "Talking like I do," he responded. "Talking like you do?" said an incredulous Morgan. "You're talking like me!" A testimony to unresolved misunderstanding, these would be the last words Al and Morgan exchanged as group leader and student.

In a final interview, Morgan was distinctly uncomfortable talking about her falling-out with Al, emphasizing that while they had "personality types that just have a natural conflict," they continued to exchange cordial greetings. When I played back the tape of their discussion of Black English, however, she provided indications of a lingering miscommunication. What Al was trying to say, she surmised, was that "for years and years, you know, black people weren't allowed to come to school, so, you know, [they were] just systematically denied the opportunity to buy into the mainstream culture." As she listened to Al charge that "acting black" means speaking the way he does, Morgan mused that perhaps he was feeling ashamed of his native variety of the language and the attendant assumption that "because you use Black English . . . you're dumber." Although saddened by his rejection, Morgan was inattentive to the possibility that Al had ambivalent feelings about "buying into the mainstream culture," or that he felt both proud and defensive about his linguistic background.

Kalie

Al's move was accomplished with quiet tact—Susan Williams explained to Kalie that Al wished to switch to her group, and one morning Kalie casually asked him if he would like to join them. That morning, he shared a paper that he had written about how he had been stereotyped at DPU—by the students who assumed he was a gangster, by local whites who seemed to regard him as a suspicious outsider, and by Morgan, who "tested" him to see if he was "as intelligent as the normal white student":

> [She] always look on me to have an insight on every topic that comes up in the group hour. Because I'm the only black student in the group doesn't mean that I am always going to have something to say, half the time I don't feel like saying anything so I don't, but my leader still calls on me. It's not a problem that I can't handle but sometimes you have so much to worry about you don't want to be bothered. When I do give my insight I make sure that I make the leader think of me as an exception to the dumb, gangster stereotype that has been put on me.

Kalie listened politely and made a few suggestions about surface structure, but avoided comment on the content. Only later in the day, when she ran into me in the campus library, did she express her amazed outrage at this essay "trashing group leaders."

In an end-of-term interview, Kalie admitted that she initially was concerned that Al might develop "an aggressive attitude, or an attitude problem against group leaders," and that she regarded his sharing of this essay as a move to "test" her. "I feel like I passed the test," Kalie added, noting that she had no misgivings about her interactions with Al aside from the fact that she "didn't have enough time." "He liked my comments," she noted repeatedly, "it's not that he didn't trust me"; and yet, she acknowledged, there was a certain distance, something that did not quite click. Perhaps, she mused, Williams should have given her more information about Al when he first moved into her group; perhaps if she were not so busy attending to her other students, she would have thought to ask.

From the beginning, Kalie had trouble remembering even the most basic facts about Al. Another African-American student, Frank, already belonged to her group, and for the duration of the semester, she habitually got them mixed up: "I always want to call Frank 'Al,'" she remarked one morning to the three fair-skinned members then present, adding, with apparent facetiousness, "I wonder why." Even in an end-of-term interview, Kalie was confused about who was who, assuming at first that Al's apparent lack of motivation was due to a commitment to athletics: "I think part of it," she mused, "is that he grew up with athletes being really important in his family. And he's in athletic teams now, and he misses . . ." I interrupted to ask which teams she thought Al played on: "I don't remember exactly," she replied, "he's, like, on baseball and basketball, something like that. He's, like, on a couple." In fact, Frank played on DPU's baseball team and had often used away games as an excuse for missing Kalie's group; Al did not play sports.

By the time Al joined Kalie's group, her tendency to launch into extensive monologues was already well established. One morning, soon after he joined her group, Kalie talked at length about big companies' mistreatment of the drug problem, and then playfully scolded Al for staring blankly into space. It would become a pattern: as Kalie delivered impassioned speeches, Al would drift into silent daydreams, interrupted only by her eventual order to "wake up!" "He never quite joined the group," Kalie admitted:

He wasn't quite as involved, because of the problem which he saw with Morgan—which, I think he had a point, but I think he also blew it up because of personal issues he has with his mother . . . then he switched groups . . . and even though he'd show up, he, like, would sit a little further away sometimes, or he'd sit at the table and be kind of half-asleep, you know, kind of like half-joking to be half-sleeping, but still, just not quite as enthusiastic. And I think part of it is that, you know, it's not that he ever had a problem, but I think that the enthusiasm and participation in the group, you know, lots of it gets going in the beginning and carries forward . . . People that come in later, it's a little harder to get them involved.

Indeed, Kalie and the other group members clearly regarded Al as an outsider—and although they were cordial in his presence, they often took advantage of his absences to engage in private asides. During the process of rushing for his fraternity, Al tried out three different hairstyles, and the other group members often joked about his changing image as they observed him from across the room. Al was absent when the group talked about writing reviews of the Spike Lee film *Do the Right Thing,* and one student felt free to remark that the way the characters spoke "is so uneducated"; when Kalie asked who the students thought might enjoy the film, another white student responded, "a black person." Al was also absent a few days later when the group discussed the pros and cons of capital punishment. In maintaining that life imprisonment provided the more severe punishment, Kalie invoked an argument that Al may well have regarded as racist: "My thing is, if you imprison somebody, they're gonna have to live with that the rest of their lives. And if they're not big black guys, they're gonna have big black guys after their asses."

On the one hand, Kalie wished to be supportive of Al's struggles, even pausing in one of our conversations to applaud the fact that he had "stood up" to Morgan:

And I really think that makes a difference with the way ethnics, especially blacks—blacks even more than Hispanics sometimes— are treated in schools. That you need to be able to stand up, be assertive, and stop something if you see it as being wrong. And I think that came up in his writing in some ways, too.

On the other hand, she was concerned about his growing solidarity with other African Americans, privately criticizing his decision to join an ethnic fraternity. Kalie also saw evidence of cultural separatism in Al's tendency to share his rough drafts only with Frank:

He and Frank—real friendly, both of them, but, but going and sitting at another table right next to us, you know . . . It's not, you know, he's not aggressively, you know, black-groups-only type of situation . . . he's not there yet. But I do see that potential a little bit. And I think that could hold him back, because I have seen that sometimes where people get, you know, a slightly bitter, you know, pro-themselves, pro-their-group attitude, the rest are the enemy. And if they're not careful, they won't do as well in school, because they spend all their time playing . . . And that could cause problems if he doesn't, you know, get into a situation that would be helpful for him in handling it, because if you think about how many people wind up getting involved in groups that they really don't, that don't help their academics, that wind up separating them from the mainstream academia, and that could be a problem.

Besides the attitudinal problems that Kalie saw as inherent to cultural separatism, she also worried that if Al associated mainly with members of his own ethnic group, he would never overcome some of the "grammar problems" in his speech and writing:

Now that's been one of the problems, is that they're really, if their friends are in a certain social group—Al's not as bad as some—but Hispanics and blacks, sometimes they speak in colloquialisms among their friends and among their social groups, and if they don't, you know, interact enough with other groups, they're not really gonna be able to speak better, and speaking better does make a big difference in how they can see their mistakes in their writing.

While "not as much" a problem with Al, Kalie had noted the "heavy accent that comes through" in the writing of some of her other African-American students—and though she allowed that "it's real colorful writing sometimes," she cautioned that "you know that grammar is not going to make it, or cut it, you know, when you get into certain teachers that are going to demand a higher academic style. And academic English is not spoken English—it's not even our spoken English."

Perspective on the Adjunct Sessions

Ironically, although Kalie seemed to attach the far greater stigma to his cultural and linguistic background, Al much preferred her to Morgan. When I asked him for a progress report after his initial meeting with Kalie, he produced a verbal collage of negative recollections about Morgan, various worries that extended outside the context of the small groups, and, finally, a few upbeat comments about Kalie:

> It's not like I have a quick attitude or anything, but *[begins to sound worn thin]* when I hear about things, you know, happening, like people calling me late at nighttime and it's something happening back home, you know, and, when I come in, to constantly get bothered, and bothered, I really, you know, I really just can't take it, you know? *[shakes head, sighs in exasperation]* You know how someone constantly nags you, and you just feel like you're just breaking on that person, but, you know *[laughs]*, you try not to. That's, that's what happened with my buddy, you know I came, we came up here, to get, trying to get away from the quick attitude, you know, and the quick tempers, and jumping down people's backs, you know, jumping on people's backs. But that's why I talk to Ms. Williams so I could get out of group. Now, okay, Kalie *[upbeat]*. I like, just by having, just by being with her one day, you know, I think that she'll make, she'll make a great group leader for me.

Even at the end of the semester, Al had little more to say about Kalie. She had been an effective group leader, he observed, although somewhat prone to "goofing off": "Kalie's a good leader, I like her, you know, when we talked about the essays, but when people would get her, when they'd sidetrack her, then she'd be sidetracked out of class. But other than that, you know, everything was fine." Al admitted, however, that the three-hour weekly time commitment had begun to seem excessive—that not enough was getting accomplished in the small groups, and that he had gradually lost interest. While he began the semester by attending Morgan's group fairly regularly, his attendance dropped markedly after he switched to Kalie's group. Overall, he was present for only eighteen sessions and absent for fifteen, an attendance record well below the class average.

Since Al came only occasionally to Kalie's group and almost never shared his writing with her, his praise of her work had an empty ring—an attempt, perhaps, to prove that despite his falling-out with Morgan, he could be easygoing and adaptable. Perhaps, too, he had established a comfortable distance from his new group leader, and his lack of criticism was more a sign of detachment than real satisfaction. As I played back audiotapes of some of his conversations with Kalie, he likewise pronounced each interaction "fine." When I asked if he wished that the group had had more to say about his essay on stereotyping, he replied, "No, I don't, you know, I'm not the type person to ask anybody to do anything . . . it was fine." Indeed, he added, he preferred that they *not* respond to

the content of his writing: "Because when we start talking about the . . .
I mean when people start talking about the content of something, you
know, it gets, uh, personal, and then, you know, a lot of things can go on."

His relationship with Morgan *had* gotten personal, and "a lot of things"
were still "going on" as he reflected back on his several weeks in her
group. Al spoke angrily of Morgan's tendency to act "like she was my
mother," but he had even more to say when I played back their discussion
of Black English:

> I don't, you know, I really don't care what Morgan has to say. She
> acts like she know everything, but she doesn't, you know. She grew
> up, she, she's an African American, but she still don't understand
> the concept of what I was trying to say. Just going back into my old
> neighborhood, talking, if she was to go back and talk the way she
> talks—she's talking about how she know how to talk black, black
> language, or, you know, whatever—even, even the Black English
> she know, wouldn't get her through, where I'm from, you know.
> You can tell that she's faking it. You don't come at people like that,
> you know, where I'm from . . . Where, you know, it really gets them
> deep, they don't like people coming in, knowing that they're not
> from the neighborhood, you know, just coming in, acting like they
> can fit in. And they take that real personal.

Al took particular exception to Morgan's use of the term *dialect* to
describe how she adjusted her linguistic style to fit various audiences:

> She always talk like she "could change her dialect"—well, maybe
> she can change her dialect around her white friends, but from the
> moment I, I met her, you know, she, she tried to be in with me and
> everything, you know—talk to me like she, she know how to talk to
> me. You know, she just talking, that's all, she just talking. She don't
> know—she don't understand.

Al was offended by Morgan's implication that she already possessed the
same sort of linguistic flexibility that he was struggling to attain:

> She was talking to me . . . like she knew where, like she know where
> I was from—like she'd been there, she grew up there, but she left and
> went to college and now she know how to talk, you know, both
> ways. No, um—maybe she knows some, some Black English, well,
> maybe she thinks she knows some Black English, she can talk, I
> guess, but she still didn't understand what I was saying. You know,
> she can't come into my, my neighborhood talking the Black English
> she knows, no time, you know. And that's how she was, just like she

knew better, like she knew what was going on back home. It's like up here—when I'm, like, around black people around here, like from Dover Park, because I have friends in Dover Park I see everyday, and when I talk Black English, they don't understand what I'm talking about, so I know she wouldn't understand. You know, if I just broke down and started talking to her, she wouldn't know what I was talking about . . . It's just a different . . . The Black English she's probably talking about is like, "yeah, dude, yeah man." That's not Black English.

Although Kalie held far more negative assumptions about Al's cultural and linguistic background than did Morgan, he somehow found her less threatening; indisputably different, she was also relatively uninterested and detached. Al could deal with her in a way that he could not deal with Morgan, who did not seem to understand where their similarities left off, who did not accept his proud self-reliance or fierce need for privacy. Even as Morgan tried to make contact and understand where he was coming from, Al was finding the gaps in her understanding unforgivable, especially where they led her to call public attention to his linguistic background.

By semester's end, Al had pulled back into a close association with African Americans from backgrounds similar to his own, speaking with renewed vigor of their cultural and linguistic bond. Some—Kalie and Morgan, for instance—would call it separatism, but Al was undeniably strengthened. Much of his vulnerability was gone, replaced by a cordial but marked detachment, and a profound lack of interest in programs that campus whites had devised to ease his passage.

Endnotes

1.   Tragically, Al's words proved prophetic: a few months after the conclusion of data collection, his brother was killed in a gang-related incident on a Southwood highway.

2.   See chapter 3 for an account of the campuswide response to the incident.

3.   Written by Rachel L. Jones, a twenty-six-year-old reporter for the *St. Petersburg Times,* the piece was first published as a *Newsweek* "My Turn" column on December 27, 1982. It was reprinted in the essay anthology that Williams was using as a class text (*Viewpoints,* edited by W. Royce Adams, published by D.C. Heath).

8 Christian

Cultural and Linguistic Background

Christian's hometown was located in a Salvadoran war zone, an area of the Morazán province largely controlled by the leftist rebels of the FMLN. Although he believed that the Salvadoran military was guilty of grievous offenses, he also held that the rebels were "as bad as the army." The FMLN had forcibly recruited a number of his former classmates, killing a few who had resisted. One night, they had come into his house and taken his stepfather, a religious man whose main concerns were tending his farm and caring for his growing family. "We never heard from him again," Christian said softly, recalling how he and his mother eventually learned from a local FMLN leader that his stepfather had been killed. "'We buried him, over there,'" the man had said, pointing to a distant blue mountain.

Concerned for Christian's safety, his family arranged for him to go live with an aunt who had established a home in the United States. When I met Christian, he had been away from El Salvador less than three years, and although he missed his family (especially a younger brother, whose name we adopted as his pseudonym), he was managing remarkably well—mastering English, earning enough money to send generous sums back home, and meeting lots of new people. Most of his campus friends were Anglo, and they teased him about his ambition to earn a doctorate in Spanish and teach at the university level. He would love to convince them, he said with an affable grin, of the value of learning his language:

> I would like to teach Anglos to become, you know, to learn the language, to learn Spanish, because Spanish is great, I like it. It's not because it's my language, but it seems to me like ... there is a need for Anglos to learn Spanish. Because you know many people, they are, like, Latinos, and they do need to become bilingual. I mean, there is a need for Anglos to become bilingual. It's not like they have to, but I mean, if they are bilingual, I mean, it's better for them. So I would like to work with Anglos.

When Christian first arrived in the United States as a high school junior, he knew almost no English, his only prior introduction being a smattering of undemanding and ineffective grammar courses. Since his new high school was 35 percent Hispanic and his aunt's family spoke Spanish at home, he worried initially that his progress would be slow. By anyone's standards, it had proved anything but slow: by the time Christian was attending his fourth ESL class a few semesters later, he was concurrently tackling college-preparatory courses which assumed facility in reading and writing English prose. Though admittedly ill-prepared for such rigors, Christian was surprised to find that he was holding his own.

Of the four focal students, Christian perhaps best fit the profile of what Ogbu (1978) has called "immigrant" minorities—that is, he did not fear assimilation, he felt no need to define himself in opposition to the dominant culture, and he measured his progress against that of less fortunate friends and relatives back home. He felt rather upbeat about his progress; and while his standard of living may have seemed meager by U.S. standards, he reveled in his new ability to provide money for the education of his brothers and sisters. Christian had experienced great losses, and he wore at times an air of deep sadness—when he spoke of his father's early death, his stepfather's murder, and his separation from his beloved younger brother—but he also seemed to be meeting each new challenge with cheerful optimism. He felt no need to defend his cultural or familial loyalties, speaking of all Salvadorans as "my poor people," and his younger brother as "my baby." His family and friends did not see Christian's academic success as "selling out," nor did they regard his new life in the United States as a threat to his cultural identity; rather, they were grateful, as he was, for the opportunities that he was exploring. His academic ambitions were part and parcel of his concern for his family: after he earned his degree, he hoped that some of his younger brothers and sisters could come live with him, completing their own educations in an atmosphere of relative safety—"because right now in El Salvador," he explained, "you, like, have to be careful with everything you do."

Adjustment to DPU

In one of his essays, Christian wrote of how he was developing the confidence to practice his still somewhat shaky English:

When I came to Summer Bridge I was a type of person that couldn't talk in class. I wouldn't start a conversation with any one. This happened because I did not have confidence in myself. I thought that because I barely could speak English at the time people were going to laugh at me or that those who spoke good English were perfect. After Summer Bridge was over, I wasn't afraid of start a conversation in English any more. When school started I became better and now with the support of my teachers and friends I am a different person. I am not the shy person I used to be.

Although he was content with his linguistic growth and primarily Anglo social network, Christian bristled at the occasional accusation that his choice of friends reflected a racist "preference." In one of his essays, he recalled being approached recently by a fellow Hispanic student:

A week ago, while I was working in the cafeteria, a Hispanic girl came to me and said, "You're a racist."
"What?"
"You're a racist," she said again.
"Why?" I asked.
"Because you only hang around with white people," she answered.
"What do you want me to do? We are only four Hispanic guys living on campus. Do you want me to hung around all the time with them? If I don't have white friends I won't succeed here," I said to her. My friends I have are whites. I am a racist, but that's no true. My best friend in Dover Park is black, my buddies in [his aunt's community] are Mexicans and Salvadoreans. I don't choose my friends because the color! What I see in people is their interior, the way they act, think, and see the world. I can care less about their color!

Christian was dumbfounded by the ethnic tensions that he witnessed at DPU. Torn though it was by hatred and class consciousness, his country was a place where "everybody's the same color":

And so we don't even think about it. It doesn't bother me, like, if I am with a black person, it doesn't bother me if I am with a white person, or with a Hispanic. Because the way I see it's, like, especially in my family, they talk, like, don't put someone down. That's what my Mom says . . . "Everyone is sacred, put here by God."

Christian was thunderstruck by the casual, senseless discrimination displayed by DPU's equity and Anglo students alike. Perhaps one of the most disturbing instances was when his former roommate, a Latino who had grown up in the United States, began muttering one fall afternoon that he "hated Salvadorans." Christian spoke of the incident often, and wrote about it in one of his essays:

> The roomate I had last semester hated me so much just because I wasn't from Mexico. After I moved out, he told my other two roomates that there was no way we could get along because he was Mexican and I was Salvadorean. This happened that month (Nov. 89) when the guerrillas took over San Salvador and one thousand of innocent people were killed. So I got mad no because he had said something about me, but probably because I was concern about my people.

In the same essay, Christian noted that he had also been harassed by Anglo students:

> One day after I got home from work I decided to visit my friend, who lives at the dorms, and when I opened the door of my apartment, a white girl was walking by with her boyfriend and as she saw me she said, "Where are your papers?"
> "Excuse me?" I answered.
> "Where are your papers?" she asked one more time. This time, I didn't say anything, but my face got red and I wanted to say "It is none of your business bitch," but the girl who saw my reaction suddenly took off with her boyfriend.
> In the same way I had been discriminated by a couple of blacks too. For example, one day I was talking Spanish with one of my friends in the Book store, and one black guy walked on the other side from where we were and said, "Speak English; this is not Mexico."
> When he said this, I got really mad. First, because this is a free country and if we can speak more than one language, nobody has the right to tell us to speak only English if we don't want to do it. Second, I was not talking with him and if we were having a conversation in Spanish it was because we wanted it this way. Finally, he called us Mexicans and we are not Mexicans.

Though he greeted such evidence of discrimination with weary impatience, Christian also sensed the misunderstanding and insecurity that informed it. He firmly believed that the campus needed to discourage cultural separatism, and he saw a particular need to "create more programs where Hispanics and blacks and white people can be mixed together":

> So they can become, like, more familiar—because, you see, the way it is, Hispanics just hang around with Hispanics, blacks hang around with blacks, and whites with whites . . . some people think Hispanics and blacks can't succeed . . . that's wrong—we have the same abilities.

Despite Christian's distress at campus ethnic tensions, he emphasized his happiness at finding new friends and achieving a fair degree of academic success. Although he planned to transfer to another school at the end of the semester, he was quick to point out that he was not unhappy at DPU. Christian hoped to double-major in Spanish and Italian, and finding DPU's offerings meager in the former and nonexistent in the latter, he had made plans to attend a junior college the following year and then to move on to a larger university with a more extensive language program. He left with many happy memories—of valued friends and of his own linguistic, social, and academic growth. Although DPU had presented a host of sometimes sobering challenges, Christian moved on with renewed confidence and heightened optimism.

Struggles with Writing

In an initial interview, Christian noted that although he was beginning to feel more confident about his writing, he still felt an urgent need for further improvement:

> Before, when I just came to college, I was afraid that I wasn't going to survive. Because my English, I couldn't bring, they said you have to write just one paper, I was, like, it was like if I was gonna die. Because the reason was I couldn't express myself, to start with. I was afraid. And now, what I'm trying to get from this English class is, like, believe in myself. I know that if I try I'm gonna do it, because I've been writing papers and I've been getting good grades, not As, but I mean Bs. And I want to be able to express what I think, what I feel, my feelings, through writing. And that's what I want to accomplish. 'Cause I know I'm gonna go to take other English classes, it's gonna be harder.

Although Christian was a strong writer in his native language, he had only recently begun to write essays in English, his high school ESL classes having emphasized only oral communication. At first, he had laboriously translated his Spanish thoughts into written English, but soon found himself overwhelmed, sidetracked by countless words and phrases that seemed to have no clear equivalent. While he continued to think in Spanish when he was "just walking around campus," he had recently begun to train himself to think in English when studying or writing. "I don't know," he added with a smile, "it's confusing."

Christian felt fairly comfortable with his ability to organize and develop ideas in writing, but saw his tentative grasp of English grammar as his main stumbling block. He regularly prodded Kalie to proofread his work, and he also approached Anglo friends for help on surface features, noting that even those friends who were not particularly strong writers often provided useful feedback. At the end of the term, although course instructor Susan Williams still worried about his "second-language problems" and "awkward sentences," Christian was feeling quite satisfied with his progress:

> I think I, I have made a lot of progress, I mean, I have progressed. Because now I don't care what they said, I have to write, you know, like, essays, like when I have an essay to write for my other classes, I do it and I get good grades . . . Before, when they said that I had to write an essay, it was like, if the world was gonna end, you know. It was like, "Ohhh, how am I gonna do this and how am I gonna do that?" And like now, when they say, you know, "You're going to write an essay," I just go, "Okay, I'm just gonna do it," and I just start doing it . . . And also, I, I try, you know, to speak up—like before I just went to classes, and I just sat there and didn't say anything, you know, and stuff like that. And now, it's like when I don't agree with someone's opinions, I go, I mean, "I don't agree with you." Before, even though I didn't agree, I couldn't say anything—I was too threatened.

Even at the beginning of the semester, Christian possessed many more resources than he seemed to realize—a wealth of passionately held convictions, and a good sense of how to set them down in prose that his teachers found generally well developed. He wrote descriptive essays about his family back home, about how attitudes toward the elderly differ in Central America and the United States, and, especially, about the political situation in El Salvador. When asked to produce an essay during an hour-long class period, he could invariably find something to say, usually with a fairly high degree of proficiency. Here, for instance, is the first paragraph of an in-class essay written at midterm:

> After ten years of the civil war in El Salvador, from the coastal mangrove swamps to the high elevation cloud forests, virtually every ecosystem is in ruins. Infant mortality rates have steadily risen making El Salvador's rate the highest in Central America. (86 deaths per 1000 live births in the first year of life). Ninety-five percent of El Salvador's families make less than what is needed to meet basic needs, about 70,000 innocent people have been killed by both sides (the army and the guerrillas). For these reasons, I would like to encourage the U.S. government who is supporting Gorbachov who with the help of Fidel Castro and Daniel Ortega is sponsoring the guerrillas, to find human needs and to cut military spending to El Salvador.

Although the final sentence needed reworking, given that the piece was written under timed conditions by a student less than three years into the English language, the paragraph reflects a surprising degree of control. A few weeks later, Christian wrote an out-of-class essay on the same subject that was even more impressive. Here is the first paragraph of that piece:

> When the civil war started in El Salvador ten years ago, the U.S. government started sending money to the Salvadoran army and since then, this government has been supporting this war that has taken the lives of 80,000 people. Now, like if we haven't have enought problems with the U.S. involment in our country, many Americans who oppose the military aid to El Salvador are taking sides with the guerrillas. What this means is that the Salvadorans who want to live in peace will have to deal with the problems that these Americans will cause to the people that still are left from the never ending civil war. I don't agree with the U.S. government policy toward El Salvador, and I also disagree with these "bunch of Americans" that oppose the U.S. military aid to El Salvador, and that instead of decreasing our torments they are increasing them by taking sides with the guerrillas who commit the same atrocities that the army does.

Inevitably, Christian's writing would continue to improve as he had more exposure to written and spoken English, and more experience writing for college courses. But what particular supports did his group leader provide? This question, which defies direct or easy answers, is addressed in following sections.

Group Leader's Response: Kalie

Although Kalie habitually confused the details of Christian's back-ground, after their first several meetings she had gathered that he was fairly comfortable with the content of his essays, but was looking for help on grammar:

> Actually all he needs help, probably, is with the patterning of where his grammar mistakes are coming from his original language. He actually writes long, well-developed essays, with pretty good description . . . And actually his English is, was pretty good, considering that he's just been here, you know, six years or something like that, four to six years ago . . . So probably with him it'll be mostly just patterning English, 'cause he's already moti-vated.[1]

When I asked how she would go about showing Christian how to "pattern" his English, she explained that she would begin by helping him identify patterns of error:

> So with him it's just to help him pattern the grammar, 'cause there's usually a pattern of grammar mistakes that people bring from one language into another, when they write in it, that a lot of times they don't understand the reasons. Very, very few classes that teach English actually teach the reasons behind a lot of stuff.

To help Christian identify his "pattern of grammar mistakes," Kalie explained that she would encourage him to read his work out loud so that he could "hear" his own errors. When I asked if she thought that he would be able to catch them without further explanation, she noted that "It's harder, but he can—he's getting it pretty good partly because he's a pretty good student. So his speaking English is better than some other people I've had . . . He's rather unusually good for English not being his original language."

In practice, however, Kalie's typical response was to simply proofread Christian's papers, correcting his mistakes without further explanation. Here, for instance, is her feedback on his in-class essay on El Salvador:

> Pretty good, you've got some grammar problems in it, but it's pretty good. Every once in a while you kind of back up, and you can almost, you almost get so passionate about what you're saying, that you fall back into an accent more when you write, you know? "Hopefully one day these governments will have mercy of El Salvador." Okay,

normally, when you write, you say, you know, "Hopefully one day these governments will have mercy *for* El Salvador." And "we'll start rebuilding . . ." and like, "in a short time, El Salvador will not longer exist." Should be, "will *no* longer exist."

Rather than asking what she meant by "falling into an accent" or why she suggested these changes, Christian quietly accepted her criticisms with characteristic gratitude. His only response to Kalie's suggestions was a simple acknowledgment: "I'll change it," he said.

Kalie was keenly aware that Christian was an unusually cooperative and motivated student. "Because he's real dedicated and damned bright," she believed that he would soon be writing like a native speaker—unlike "some bilingual students" who "spend all their spare time reading and speaking in Spanish." Kalie saw Christian as holding a definite advantage over Hispanic students born in the United States:

> He got plopped down here when he was like, well, he must have been eleven, twelve, something like that, between ten and thirteen, some age like that, I'm not sure, and so he got plopped into a classroom where he was embarrassed because he didn't know any English at all, and so he had to take a crash course. And because he had to take a crash course, he was highly motivated . . . Sometimes you have a higher motivation to learn it fast, because you're desperate, because you know you don't know it. And if you grow up here, and you think you know it, or good enough, and it isn't until you really get to college and it gets slapped in your face that you're not going to make the grade if you can't start working on it now, and it's awfully late to start to learn now.

By the end of the semester, Kalie was generally happy with Christian's progress, although she worried about the lingering incidence of grammatical errors in his work:

> He's made good progress, but he had pretty good writing to begin with. But I think that once in a while he lapses back—I mean, this is a big problem I see with a lot of people who have English as a second language, are grammar problems. He lapses back into his old problems, but overall, his papers have improved . . . [he's] recognizing his grammar problems and his mistakes, and . . . the biggest problem with proofing, if English is not your native language, is being able to see your mistakes . . . Not just grammatical problems, but writing problems that relate to English as a second language. It's more than just grammatical problems, sometimes it's a way you say

things. You know, it's like, if you learn English, you'll learn it either stilted or with a strange accent or with other words put in.

Kalie seemed to believe that Christian's grammar had improved largely because of her intervention:

I saw Christian's work a lot . . . and having somebody, really, you know, zoom in on his work and on a line-by-line with him there, made him really focus in on the page . . . In the beginning, when I put out a problem, he wouldn't understand what it was. You know, and he would, like, I'd have to explain the whole thing. And now, like, "Oh shit, I forgot this, didn't I?" and he'll correct it, right there, sometimes before I really had a chance to say what it was . . . I'd look at him and he'd say, "Oh, I've got the wrong verb form."

Kalie was somewhat less satisfied, however, with Christian's response to her feedback on content. Occasionally she came away feeling that she had made headway, as when she asked him a series of rapid-fire questions designed to elicit more descriptive detail in a paper that he had written about his mother. When he wrote about the war in El Salvador, however, Kalie felt stymied by Christian's persistent refusal to consider her point of view: "We disagree politically . . . Because I know, even though he lived in El Salvador, I think I know a little bit more . . . I've read political science articles and studies."

After reading one of his essays on El Salvador, she felt that he was "real emotional" about the subject, and therefore unable to benefit from her feedback. While Kalie was "trying to get him to write in such a way to really convince me with a good logical essay," she had the lingering sense that "he wasn't really doing that—he was just kind of being really rhetorical." Kalie was worried that if he continued to "block himself in other issues," he might run into problems in writing in the content areas:

If he can't clearly state it, if he gets too emotionally involved without backing off enough to be able to try to see the other person's viewpoint so he can see how to oppose it, he's not going to be able to write some papers and answer some questions as well as he might otherwise . . . is he gonna be able to, to clearly defend his viewpoint without becoming rhetorical and just not saying much other than the fact that he disagrees.

Kalie and Christian's first discussion of the situation in El Salvador occurred on the morning of Violeta Chammoro's victory over Daniel Ortega in the Nicaraguan election. Kalie was depressed, but Christian—

who despised Ortega's policy of providing arms to the leftist rebels—was elated. Even weeks later, Kalie recalled the encounter with disdain, maintaining that even though Christian was a native of the area, his knowledge could not match the "enormous amounts of information" that she had taken in through extensive reading and attendance at rallies and films. A vehement supporter of the FMLN rebels, Kalie was offended by Christian's equally vehement opposition. When I asked what she thought might account for his feelings, Kalie articulated a series of erroneous assumptions:

> His family lives in the capital, where there is a lot more safety. And they haven't lived in all the bombings that are in the countryside. And he hasn't had the contact with the FMLN, you know, he's just heard what the government's had to say . . . you know, and so I know an awful lot about the El Salvador that he doesn't really come from. And it's not that he doesn't see or know some stuff, but he's also young enough and he's also been fortunate enough, thank God, that he hasn't had to see some of that, and he hasn't had to be threatened, because, with going into the army, because he left and came here to go to school.

Kalie likened Christian's alleged tunnel vision to that of U.S. citizens who are unaware of the plight of the homeless: "he's ignorant," she charged, thumping the table, "he doesn't understand." "He has this real naive attitude" about the current regime, she continued, "'cause he lives in the city, and the city's inundated with pro-government propaganda, and is inundated with the news reports about the guerrillas, and the fact that the war's going on because of the guerrillas, you know, that type of an attitude."

While Christian wrote often about his experiences back home and talked freely about his background in interviews, Kalie did not discover the underlying reasons for his firmly held beliefs. She knew the light-hearted, playful side of Christian, not the air of weary sadness that sometimes passed over him as he spoke with me about the situation in his country. Perhaps Christian would have felt reluctant to reveal personal tragedies during the small-group meetings, but he never really had a chance to try, for his perspectives were preempted by Kalie's insistent urgency.

Although Kalie found Christian's political perspective troubling, she was generally heartened by his willingness to disagree with her. This was especially true when they discussed his writing:

He was really willing to hear problems and possible changes, and yet, sometimes he'd still say, "No, I don't want to do that" . . . you know, "Right or wrong, this is the way I want to write it." Okay, that's great, you know, because sometimes I'd state, "These are grammar problems, these are suggestions." I would try to separate the two—suggestions you can throw out the window, you know.

If she sometimes seemed to be bulldozing her way through their discussions with little regard for what he was taking away, Kalie felt genuine affection for Christian, and liked to think that she had helped him feel more confident about his academic writing. As discussed in the next section, it was an assessment with which Christian would basically agree—albeit for rather different reasons.

Perspective on the Adjunct Sessions

Although Christian liked Kalie and felt that she had helped him, he did not take her as seriously as she seemed to suppose. While Kalie took a rather teacher-centered view of her work with students, apparently assuming that she alone was responsible for whatever learning took place, Christian's perception of the small-group hour was far more inclusive. He valued the group as a community of friends, and although Kalie sometimes prodded them to do their work, he basically saw her as just another member:

She's like a friend—she is like a friend. It's just the way I see her. When I go there I don't see her, like, of course, I have to respect her, like, as a teacher. But I just, I didn't even think of she being like a teacher. I think she's just like one more person there, like a friend. That's the way I see her, she's like a friend. Because the way she made us feel like, we discuss things, and other kinds of issues. And that's great.

Partly because Kalie's outspokenness made them feel free to express opinions, Christian explained, the group members had grown into a close and supportive community. As a fairly recent immigrant, Christian found their discussions enlightening and their friendship heartening:

We help each other. We help . . . we talk, I mean, you know, like, of issues, you know, that we discuss things, and it's like, I don't know. There are things that I don't know. I haven't been living in this country for that long, and so this way I go "oh!" And so they help me to analyze, and to see, reality, to explore, you know, things that

> I didn't know before. And so it's like we discuss. They made me feel like, made me feel like we're family, too, like, you know, like they're part of my life.

As opposed to the whole-class setting, where Christian was usually hesitant about speaking up, the small group provided a comfortable and accessible forum:

> You know, like, in the class we are the whole class together, and we can't, um, arg- . . . I mean, you can't, it's like, we got the opinion of the whole class and in small group we can discuss, like, as a small group, the way we see it. We have more chance, like, more opportunity to talk. And in class it's, like, one people talk, and then you . . . there are more people and therefore less opportunity to express ourselves.

Since Christian had been habitually shy about speaking up in group settings, he found the small-group experience groundbreaking:

> Probably the group has helped to speak up, you know, like not be afraid of anything because, you know, Kalie, ah, she talks a lot, all the time, everything. She's like, I don't know, but she's cool. And so she make you feel like, you know, if you want to say something, you know, say it, you know, and better to say something than to keep it to yourself. So probably the small groups helped me to speak up.

The group sessions helped Christian with "confidence and all that":

> To help people to become better at writing, you have to, you know, help people to socialize and stuff like that . . . 'cause, like, if you socialize with people, you know, you ask them, and you know, it's like, "What do you think about this and what do you think about that?" in my writing or stuff. And they give you feedback. And so if you don't talk with people, you don't have anyone to talk to, ask for. And the guys who are, like, in my group, I ask them, you know, "What do you think about this?" Like, out of class I call them, you know.

Indeed, Christian began to regard the adjunct group as primary: "Ms. Williams, you know, she reinforces," he explained, noting that Kalie and the other group members offered "more detail." He was almost never absent, and by semester's end, he sometimes attended only the adjunct component, skipping the regular class. "I feel, like, it's better, like, to get help in group from, like, three people," he explained.

There were, he allowed, times when the group "didn't talk about anything about class," falling into off-task chatter on a range of topics, usually instigated by Kalie ("she just, you know, went nuts talking about her life and other stuff like that"). Notwithstanding the value that he saw in the group's more freewheeling discussions, he often longed for a more focused approach—and, particularly, more attention to his written products. Although Kalie assumed that she had helped Christian improve his grasp of English grammar through close readings of his work, he felt that such attention was lacking. When she did look at his essays, he was grateful for any feedback that she provided—be it a barrage of open-ended questions, simple correction of grammatical errors, or, for that matter, heated disagreement with his ideas.

By midterm, Christian had come to feel that he and Kalie were able to disagree without being disagreeable. When I played back one of their discussions of the situation in Central America, he laughed heartily: "we got into this big argument," he finally said, seeming to enjoy the memory. Since Kalie had repeatedly overruled him and cut him off, I asked what he would have liked to have said to her. Christian's words, though forceful, were spoken without evident rancor:

> She didn't know anything about it! You know, she's like, I mean, sure she knows what she reads from newspapers. But as I said before [in the conversation in the group], who writes the newspapers? Are they really into it, I mean, do they just write because somebody tell them, somebody tells them what's going on? And you know, I mean, or do they really see what's going on? . . . Yeah. It's like, you know, they just talk. And just because they read the newspaper or whatever, but they haven't been there, you know. They, they haven't experienced—uh, those people who go, they just go to San Salvador, if they go, they just go to somewhere, you know, where they don't see *anything,* like, they don't see how things are. You know what I mean? They don't go to Morazán—I'm pretty sure they don't go, to Morazán, and see how guerrillas, what guerrillas do and stuff like that.

Christian was unaware that Kalie assumed that he had grown up in San Salvador, that she took him for the sheltered child of a privileged family. If he had known, he probably would have forgiven her this, too—for even in the above quote, he soon moved from his disagreement with Kalie, arguing instead with an impersonal "them." Christian demonstrated a quiet strength in his relationship with Kalie—or perhaps, to some extent, he discovered it there. In the small group, Christian was secure enough to express his ideas and listen to hers, undaunted by their sometimes sharp disagreements, neither swayed from his convictions nor moved to lasting anger. For him, the newfound ability to speak up was primary—the value of the group located not in whether he convinced anyone, but in the very opportunity to argue.

The experience of Kalie's group was one of many satisfying memories that Christian would take away from his year at DPU: "I just liked—I liked her," he said at the conclusion of a final interview. Though she had sometimes spoken with the voice of authority, Christian had found Kalie too quirky and eccentric ever to come across as officious. She helped him become a better writer—but not, as they had both anticipated in the beginning, through careful coaching on the fine points of English grammar. Through their friendship and free-spirited conversations, Christian had become more comfortable with both his oral and written discourse; and although Kalie's stance can be seen as problematic in some respects, she had—perhaps unintentionally—provided assistance of fundamental value. Somewhat ironically, Christian came to see their occasional dissonance as central to their collaboration, and his group's arguments as central to their sense of community. His willingness to join the fray was an essential part of his emerging self-confidence, of a ripening ability to enjoy the play of divergent ideas.

Endnote

1. As noted earlier, Christian had actually lived in the United States less than three years.

IV Conclusion

For the beginning is assuredly the end—since we know nothing, pure and simple, beyond our own complexities.

—William Carlos Williams, *Paterson*

9 The Continuing Challenge

Borders into Boundaries: An Elusive Transformation

This research report began with the promise of a long and perhaps disconcerting look at one writing program's role in accommodating linguistic and cultural pluralism. It has been a story of a rich and somewhat troubled period of transition—of good intentions only partially fulfilled, of complexities left unattended, and of the vulnerabilities of students and beginning instructors as they struggled to find paths through unfamiliar and often arduous terrain. I also began with reference to Erickson's (1987) argument that teachers of culturally diverse students must work to transform politically charged "borders" into neutralized "boundaries": a goal, this story suggests, that can easily remain as elusive as it is lofty, particularly for those still new to the instructional role, and still unaware that they, too, are infected with the instinctive tendency to cast difference as deficit.

Lacking ongoing guidance and opportunities for conversation about their work, the group leaders did not seem particularly reflective about linguistic and cultural variation, nor did they grasp the importance of defusing its attendant politics. Occupying an institutional context where few displayed much curiosity about the precise needs of nonmainstream students, they were generally unable to see the many points at which their work intersected with other levels of meaning—with these students' linguistic and cultural backgrounds, with the history of their struggles with writing, and with their attempts to adjust to life at this predominantly Anglo campus. In this inadequate conceptualization of their task, these peer teachers reflected larger patterns of misapprehension, of issues that extended beyond the confines of the adjunct sessions or basic writing class, into the institutional and societal contexts that contained them. Like all novice educators, Kalie and Morgan needed to develop ways of seeing, ways of inquiring that would lead them to the requisite understandings. For this they needed models: of what it means to approach their work with ethnographers' eyes for individual difference, to be ever watchful for

169

ways to build from the resources that students already possess, and to problematize their assumptions about who these students are and what they need.

In an era of shrinking resources and demands for accountability, even the most seasoned among us are often tempted to skate upon the glossy surface of good intentions, to avoid the vulnerability that is part and parcel of candid reflection. Contemplating the gap between the ideal visions in our heads and their flawed instantiations too often means becoming open to charges of ineptitude and, even, to reductions in institutional support and given that basic writing programs are so often ghettoized to begin with—begrudgingly funded and staffed by temporary part-timers—it is unsurprising that talk of doubts and conflicts often takes a back seat to tales of "what works for me." No wonder that we so often turn, as did faculty and administrators at DPU, to hopeful rhetoric: "providing quality education to students who are from groups historically underrepresented in higher education . . . and meeting and addressing the needs of these students." Ironically, such resolutions have a way of turning inside out, of becoming not the pathways that we imagine, but a mirage, a camouflage (Hull and Rose 1990).

Consider, for instance, what it meant to say that this program was "serving the needs of linguistic minorities," or that Sylvia, Christian, Fannie, and Al belonged to such a subcategory. Certainly the label conceals much more than it reveals, prompting talk among teachers and group leaders of "first-language interference," "patterns of grammatical error," and "lingering ESL problems." All four focal students sometimes departed from mainstream English grammar, and some attention to surface features was certainly in order; but in each case, to assume that such concerns were of the essence is to miss more fundamental understandings. These students were not simply acquiring new linguistic "skills"—they were looking as well for a way to belong, struggling to balance their emerging membership in the campus community against older memberships and loyalties. At times the group leaders managed to engage their students, to balance personal warmth and high expectations, to learn enough about their students to understand their present needs; more often, though, these leaders conceptualized their work as filling empty vessels, forgetting that they, too, were in a powerful position to learn—that their job involved not only hastening change in others, but also being changed themselves.

So, too, was the campus caught half-unknowingly in a disorienting dialectic. Even as it was seeking to transform equity students into mainstream achievers, DPU was slowly awakening to the fact that the process of change was a reciprocal one—and that like the students, the school could never quite return to its former self, having already set in motion an institutional metamorphosis as unpredictable as it was inexorable.

Beyond Good Intentions

As campuses across the country continue to struggle with the challenge of student diversity, this examination of DPU's basic writing adjunct program makes the following general recommendations:

Conflicts attending equity programs must not remain tacit; rather, they should serve as the impetus for needed debate and reflection.

Many of the tensions chronicled in chapter 3 represent legitimate, substantive, and increasingly widespread concerns: How to open wide the door but also keep standards high? How to encourage cultural pride but discourage cultural separatism? How to reach out with personal warmth and an eagerness to help while also encouraging students to assume responsibility for their own learning? These are serious questions deserving of serious attention, not appealing slogans or insistence that all is well. As individuals and as institutions, we must not only acknowledge the tensions in our thinking, but realize their value in framing discussions of how to improve upon current efforts. We as a nation will continue to grapple with our emerging diversity for years to come, and educators will have key voices in ongoing, often politically charged, debates.

As Americans, we prefer to believe in our commitment to equality and justice for all, and many of us grow a bit uncomfortable in the face of real injustice or, for that matter, real difference. Increasingly, to say that someone has committed the act of "stereotyping" is to assign a scarlet letter, an invitation to admire the distance between a broad-minded "us" and narrow-minded "them." Attention to discrimination must be accompanied by an awareness that we are all somehow implicated—that we all hold ethnocentric biases, that we all have trouble understanding people who are different, and that we all tend to think that to be unlike us is to be somehow less. In addition to free discussion at the institutional level, we need the courage and honesty to examine the assumptions and biases tha we hold as individuals.

Before we can hope to provide novice educators with the neede models, we must become better acquainted with our own struggle to fin firm footing on this shifting terrain, reflecting together upon the inevi table unevenness of our work, upon our occasional self-doubts, and upo our ongoing search for ways to provide appropriate assistance—this often, while dealing with the constraints of crowded schedules, limite budgets, and institutional environments that sometimes provide less than-adequate support.

- *Accommodating diversity must be seen as everybody's concern.*

As noted in chapter 3, while DPU's faculty voiced unanimous suppor for the campus's equity goals, many believed that the responsibility fo supporting nontraditional students rested solely with special program like the Comprehensive Learning Project (CLP) and Educational Oppor tunity Program (EOP). As the Academic Vice-President pointed out beyond being "nice and nonbigoted," most faculty did not see themselve as particularly implicated in the many changes that the campus wa undergoing.

As tenured faculty remained essentially unchanged by the campus' transformation, equity programs were perennially stigmatized, com monly regarded as nonacademic exercises in "handholding." There wa grumbling all around that these students were not becoming fully profi cient writers at the conclusion of their two semesters in the CLP, and on academic department set in place a policy barring from its courses an students who had not yet passed freshman composition. On one recen morning, as a CLP basic writing course brainstormed argumentativ papers in animated small groups, a professor from a neighboring class room stormed in and confronted the instructor, angrily complaining tha the noise was disturbing her more "serious" class.

When professors ask diverse students to write term papers or essa exams for these "serious" courses, they come face to face with the academic ramifications of educational equity—and quite possibly, wit conflicts in their own commitment to meeting and addressing these students' varied needs. No basic writing class can prepare students lik Fannie, Sylvia, Al, or Christian to write like native speakers of main stream English, and no basic writing course can provide a definitive pass into the discourse community of a particular discipline. Insistence that "I treat all my students the same" is not enough, for to treat these students fairly may mean approaching them with special sensitivities and strategies. Inevitably, their need for support will endure far beyond what programs like the CLP and EOP can do in the early semesters. Faculty in the disciplines must wrestle with the question of what sort of continuing support is appropriate, and how best to provide it.

- *Programs and policies must be informed by careful attention to the needs of individual students.*

As we come to know basic writers better, Mina Shaughnessy once observed, "we begin to see that the greatest barrier to our work with them is our ignorance of them" (1976, 238). Regardless of recent calls to "attend to individual differences" and "build from what students bring," this study suggests some of the ways in which Shaughnessy's observation remains apt, especially as the goals and rationales of "basic writing" programs become increasingly entangled with equity policies. Before peer teachers can "collaborate" within diverse students' "zones of proximal development" (Vygotsky 1978), they must first understand who these students are and what they need—linguistically, socially, and academically. Before peer teachers can effectively adjust the "scaffolds" that they have constructed (Bruner 1978; Applebee and Langer 1983, 1986), they must develop a watchful eye for how students are changing over time, observing their appropriation of yesterday's lessons and readiness for tomorrow's.

While the adjunct program was ostensibly intended to "individualize instruction," one of the most significant shortcomings of the group leaders' work with students was their lack of attention to how students' backgrounds were shaping their current needs. Similarly, many of DPU's administrators and faculty spoke of "underprepared" or "ethnic minority" students as if they somehow were a cohesive group, designing programs and charting policies uninformed by attention to the rich variety that such labels mask. When the chair of one campus educational equity subcommittee suggested inviting students to its meetings, the idea struck many as distinctly novel; so, too, was the case when the Dean of Students suggested interviewing equity students to gather their perspectives on the campus experience.

Perhaps partly why programs like the CLP are often ghettoized is because the varied needs that they are attempting to meet are so commonly underestimated. Even as it approaches cliché status, "individualized instruction" remains a slogan more readily invoked than realized.

- *Educators' reflections upon their work with all students—including those who are linguistic minorities—must be informed by understandings from the theoretic and research literature.*

Only half-jokingly, a group leader described her switch from a "directive" to a "collaborative" mode as abandoning her old practice of "telling them what I want them to do" to "asking the questions to lead them to what I want them to do"; a writing program administrator who had forgotten the work of Flower and Hayes (1981a, 1981b) described the writing process as a linear sequence—"prewrite, write, revise." If the slogans sounded current—"collaborate, don't evaluate," "teach writing as a process, not a product"—the approaches often were not. Rather than revolutionary new ways of thinking about the teaching and learning of writing, the "collaborative learning" and "process" banners gestured toward collections of isolated "how to's."

Real reform happens when educators' thinking is transformed, when classroom changes are informed by understandings not only from day-to-day experience, but also from the empirical and theoretic literature. Lacking such grounding, "innovative" programs can bear remarkable similarity to old-fashioned ones. Like all educators, those who work with culturally and linguistically diverse students must be encouraged to envision their craft as more than a collection of classroom strategies unconnected to a larger conceptual frame. Although the group leaders' desire for autonomy was understandable, it was also premature, reflecting the campuswide tendency to underestimate the importance and difficulty of their work. Like any professionals, they needed both initial training and ongoing input from colleagues. Given the stature of the challenges before them, the question of "what group leaders need to know" deserved rich and multiplex answers; their push for autonomy was perhaps better put on hold until their own professional learning had been more abundantly scaffolded.

Opportunities to read and discuss relevant literature are certainly a beginning, but novice educators must also find a way to locate their own experiences within these new understandings. The teacher-researcher movement is providing a promising new start in that direction, but more attention is needed to the question of how to help both new and experienced educators bridge this gap.

- *Like all students, equity students must be supported in their efforts to find personal meaning in academic work.*

For Christian, a strong and experienced writer in his native language, academic writing was already a meaning-making activity, providing opportunities to present his points of view on matters of pressing personal concern; on the other hand, when Al, Sylvia, and Fannie were asked to write anything other than personal narratives, they felt stymied and unengaged. All three needed help in building bridges between the pleasures of private conversation and the rigors of public prose, help in seeing how issues that arose from their varied experiences might segue into avenues of academic pursuit (see DiPardo 1990a, 1990b).

Before they had a chance to learn much about these students' histories and convictions, the group leaders tried to nudge them toward an emphasis upon written products; "What's your thesis?" opened many a brainstorming discussion, denying students the luxury of the yet-yeasty hunch. When students faced time-restricted midterm and final exams, this movement away from writing as meaning making became even more pronounced, as form took even greater precedence over function. Writing remained essentially something one does, if somewhat unsatisfactorily, for a teacher.

Small-group instruction certainly holds the potential to chisel away at this traditional conception of writing, but that effect is far from automatic. Group leaders can easily default into the only mode of instruction that many of them have ever witnessed, replicating a teacher-centered classroom under this "student-centered" guise. Students may decline even the most well-meaning ministrations of adjunct staff and fellow group members, making an existential choice to refrain from sharing their writing (and, by extension, themselves); or, like Sylvia and Al, students may decide that they trust friends more than the members of their assigned groups, discovering more appropriate help outside the classroom.

Not everyone will respond with Christian's willingness to regard his group as a supportive, if sometimes contentious, community of fellow writers, and certainly this sort of trust cannot be mandated by programs. On the other hand, when group leaders work within a context where attentiveness to learners' needs is the rule rather than the exception, they are more likely to foster the kinds of interactions that will help students discover a sense of personal engagement in their academic writing. While educators should respect students' needs for privacy, they must also be unflaggingly attentive to what students are willing to offer, and to use these offerings as a starting point, a foundation.

Like the best writing, the best talk about writing is reciprocally charge
with personal meaning—alternately serious and playful, purposeful an
experimental, but forever predicated upon faith in the receptivity of th
other. Whether the audience be crankily argumentative or gently support
ive, a writer has to care enough about what she or he has to say to perforr
that intrinsically social act of reaching out with words, of bridging th
territory that separates "them" from "me." The process involves trust i
both oneself and one's audience, the sort of trust that provides the courag
to expose one's awkward first steps, to heatedly disagree, or, perhaps, t
revise one's ideas and words in response to a reader's dissent. Engage
ment, trust, the shared making of meaning: these were as fundamental t
DPU's basic writers as to all writers.

Another Chapter

As this project drew to a close, DPU remained in the throes of unresolve
tensions, its veneer of interracial harmony periodically stripped away a
campus controversies came and went. Soon after the conclusion of dat
collection, a group of African-American students responded to what the
considered a racist cartoon in the school newspaper by staging a paper-
burning ceremony in the central quad. The editor termed the event "an
unacceptable act of censorship," and in the weeks that followed, the pages
of the campus paper were filled with angry accusations—including the
charge that the Black Student Union was a haven for "hysteria-driven
fanatics." More recently, the campus's equity policy again came under
suspicion when a highly visible African-American student was charged
with participating in a series of local and statewide crimes. His alleged
collaborator was a member of an inner-city street gang, and the county
newspaper ran a series of articles exploring the possible gang connections
of other DPU equity students. "Dover Park law enforcement officials say
members of [inner-city] street gangs attend DPU and officials know it,"
one article noted; meanwhile, DPU's President refused to comment,
brushing aside such charges by insisting that the question of gang
membership was simply "irrelevant" to what these students were trying
to accomplish in college. "But it is relevant," countered the editor of the
campus newspaper, noting that the possible presence of gang members on
campus was "like lifting a corner of a picturesque snapshot and finding
something dark and scary underneath." "I don't want to look at my

classmates and wonder," he mused, "but in light of the recent headlines, I can't help but wonder." Every African-American and Hispanic male had come to be regarded as a de facto suspect, and tensions ran high among DPU's entire equity-student population.

In the troubled weeks that followed, one CLP instructor—a middle-aged man who had been a prominent student activist back in the 1960s—inadvertently dramatized the campus's colliding ideals. One morning he walked into his office to find one of his brightest African-American students near tears, a copy of the campus newspaper unfolded on her lap. She told him that the campus was a terrible place, that she would be leaving for good at the end of the semester, and she handed him the offending article. Although the piece struck him as less inflammatory than some that the paper had run of late, he was deeply disturbed by her reaction, regarding it as yet another manifestation of the campus's growing racial unrest. Later that morning, he walked over to see the paper's faculty adviser, relating his concern and suggesting that a student advisory board be set up to discuss the kinds of reactions that recent articles had been provoking. Incredulous, the adviser responded by asking him to repeat his name: "Are you who I think you are?" she wanted to know, remembering his radical leadership from her own student days. The next morning, his picture was on the front page of the county newspaper, beside it the headline "From Free Speech to Censorship." Just as "political correctness" was becoming a national buzzword, the CLP instructor had tapped into a central conflict at DPU—between a liberal-minded commitment to educational equity and an equally liberal-minded commitment to the free-speech rights of campus and community Anglos, many of whom were increasingly concerned about the academic and social ramifications of student diversity.

Meanwhile, a growing number of accrediting commissions were adding "progress towards multiculturalism" to their criteria, holding that today's students will be entering a world "that has no majority" (Weiner 1990, B1). If few would dispute such goals in principle, their implementation continued to be hounded by concern and dissent—dramatized not only in strident National Association of Scholars' policy statements and discussions about D'Souza's *Illiberal Education* (1991), but also in college administrators' mild-mannered worries about institutional image. "We're not going to be ranked among the country's best liberal-arts colleges if people think of us as an institution that has become truly multicultural," one president was recently quoted as saying; although "nothing is further from the truth," he allowed, "most people in this country believe that if you focus attention on equality, quality is going to suffer" (Monaghan 1990).

What accounts for the high attrition rates of equity students at DPU and campuses like it—underpreparation, economic struggle, cultural alienation, enduring cynicism about the doors that a university education might open? The best answer, one might surmise, is that it is all these and more besides; for the problem lies not within equity students alone, but within all of us who struggle to promote interracial harmony in our classrooms and on our campuses, and who wrestle with our own ethnocentric biases and deficit-oriented assumptions about students whose backgrounds differ from our own. Witness a recent survey by the National Opinion Research Center examining white Americans' attitudes toward ethnic minorities (Smith 1990): while most whites say that they oppose racial discrimination more than ever, the study revealed that many still cling to certain stereotypes about Hispanics and African Americans— that they are lazier, more prone to violence, less intelligent, and less patriotic. "This survey tells us in no uncertain terms," noted one of its designers, "that the American racial dilemma lives on" (Armstrong 1991). Following announcement of the Rodney King verdict in Los Angeles in the spring of 1992, a coalition of equity students conducted a peaceful protest march from campus to downtown, accompanied by a scattering of CLP and EOP staff, but otherwise alone in yet another attempt to register their perspectives on the continuing "racial dilemma."

Where DPU is going with this dilemma—indeed, where the country is going—is a story yet to be written. As with DPU's attempts to meet the needs of nonmainstream writers, the development and day-to-day enactment of instructional programs will be shaped by national debates of a much larger scope, and an understanding of specific instructional encounters will be increasingly dependent upon an ability to place them within these sociopolitical contexts. As administrators, teachers, and students negotiate paths through this still-vexing maze, the issues suggested by DPU's basic writing adjunct program begin to define an important agenda for practitioners and researchers alike.

References

Applebee, A. N., and J. A. Langer. 1983. Instructional scaffolding: Reading and writing as natural language activities. *Language Arts* 60:168–75.

_____. 1986. Reading and writing instruction: Toward a theory of teaching and learning. In *Review of research in education,* vol. 13, ed. E. Z. Rothkopf. Washington, D.C.: American Educational Research Association.

Armstrong, L. S. 1991. Racial, ethnic prejudice still prevalent, survey finds. *Education Week,* January 16, 7.

Astin, A. W. 1982. *Minorities in American higher education.* San Francisco: Jossey-Bass.

Bakhtin, M. 1981. *The dialogic imagination: Four essays.* Ed. M. Holquist; trans. C. Emerson and M. Holquist. Austin: University of Texas Press.

Bartholomae, D. 1985. Inventing the university. In *When a writer can't write,* ed. M. Rose, 134–65. New York: Guilford.

Beach, R. 1986. Demonstrating techniques for assessing writing in the writing conference. *College Composition and Communication* 37:56–65.

Bereiter, C., and S. Engelmann. 1966. *Teaching disadvantaged children in the preschool.* Englewood Cliffs, N.J.: Prentice-Hall.

Bizzell, P. 1986. What happens when basic writers come to college? *College Composition and Communication* 37:294–301.

Bogdan, R. C., and S. K. Biklen. 1982. *Qualitative research for education: An introduction to theory and methods.* Boston: Allyn and Bacon.

Brand, A. G. 1987. The why of cognition: Emotion and the writing process. *College Composition and Communication* 38:436–43.

Brodkey, L. 1987a. *Academic writing as social practice.* Philadelphia: Temple University Press.

_____. 1987b. Writing ethnographic narratives. *Written Communication* 4:25–50.

Bruffee, K. A. 1978. The Brooklyn plan: Attaining intellectual growth through peer-group tutoring. *Liberal Education* 64:447–68.

_____. 1984. Collaborative learning and the "conversation of mankind." *College English* 46:635–52.

Bruner, J. S. 1978. The role of dialogue in language acquisition. In *The child's conception of language,* ed. A. Sinclair, R. J. Javella, and W.J.M. Levelt, 241-56. New York: Springer-Verlag.

———. 1985. On teaching thinking: An afterthought. In *Thinking and learning skills,* ed. J. Segal, S. F. Chipman, and R. Glaser, vol. 2. Hillsdale, N.J.: Lawrence Erlbaum.

California State Department of Education. 1982. *Racial or ethnic distribution of staff and students in California public schools, 1979–80.* Sacramento: California State Department of Education.

———. 1985. *Racial or ethnic distribution of staff and students in California public schools, 1984–85.* Sacramento: California State Department of Education.

Carter, D. J., and R. Wilson. 1991. *Minorities in higher education: Ninth annual status report.* Washington, D.C.: American Council on Education, Office of Minorities in Higher Education.

Cazden, C. B. 1988. *Classroom discourse: The language of teaching and learning.* Portsmouth, N.H.: Heinemann.

Center for Education Statistics. 1986. *The condition of education: A statistical report.* Washington, D.C.: U.S. Department of Education, Office of Educational Research and Improvement.

Cintron, R. 1991. Reading and writing graffiti: A reading. *Quarterly Newsletter of the Laboratory of Comparative Human Cognition* 13:21-24.

Collision, M. N.-K. 1988. Serious issues, touchy subject: New film pokes fun at black fraternities. *Chronicle of Higher Education,* 34 (22): A34-35.

Committee on CCCC Language Statement. 1974. Students' right to their own language. *College Composition and Communication* 25(3): 1-32.

Cummins, J. 1979. Linguistic interdependence and the educational development of bilingual children. *Review of Educational Research* 49:222-51.

———. 1981. The role of primary language development in promoting educational success for language minority students. In *Schooling and language minority students: A theoretical framework,* 3-49. Los Angeles: California State University, Evaluation, Dissemination and Assessment Center.

———. 1986. Empowering minority students: A framework for intervention. *Harvard Educational Review* 56:18-36.

Deutsch, M., et al. 1967. *The disadvantaged child: Selected papers of Martin Deutsch and associates.* New York: Basic Books.

DiPardo, A. 1990a. Narrative knowers, expository knowledge: Discourse as a dialectic. *Written Communication* 7:59-95.

———. 1990b. Narrative discourse in the basic writing class: Meeting the challenge of cultural pluralism. *Teaching English in the Two-Year College* 17:45-53.

_____. 1992. "Whispers of coming and going": Lessons from Fannie. *Writing Center Journal* 12:125–44.

_____. In press. Stimulated recall in research on writing: An antidote to "I don't know, it was fine." In *Verbal reports in the study of writing,* ed. P. Smagorinsky. Newbury Park, Calif.: Sage Publications.

DiPardo, A., and S. W. Freedman. 1988. Peer response groups in the writing classroom: Theoretic foundations and new directions. *Review of Educational Research* 58:119–49.

D'Souza, D. 1991. *Illiberal education: The politics of race and sex on campus.* New York: The Free Press.

Erickson, F. 1986. Qualitative methods in research on teaching. In *Handbook of research on teaching,* 3d ed., ed. M. C. Wittrock. New York: Macmillan.

_____. 1987. Transformation and school success: The politics and culture of educational achievement. *Anthropology and Education Quarterly* 18:335–56.

_____. 1989. Learning and collaboration in teaching. *Language Arts* 66:430–41.

Erickson, F., S. Florio, and J. Buschman. 1980. *Fieldwork in educational research.* Occasional Paper no. 36. East Lansing: Michigan State University, Institute for Research on Teaching.

Fillmore, L. W. 1991. A question for early-childhood programs: English first or families first? *Education Week,* June 19, 32.

Fischer, M. J. 1986. Ethnicity and the post-modern arts of memory. In *Writing culture: The poetics and politics of ethnography,* ed. J. Clifford and G. E. Marcus. Berkeley and Los Angeles: University of California Press.

Flower, L., and J. R. Hayes. 1981a. A cognitive process theory of writing. *College Composition and Communication* 32:365–87.

_____. 1981b. Plans that guide the composing process. In *Writing: Process, development and communication,* ed. C. H. Fredericksen and J. F. Dominic, vol. 2 of *Writing: The nature, development and teaching of written communication.* Hillsdale, N.J.: Lawrence Erlbaum.

Fordham, S., and J. U. Ogbu. 1986. Black students' school success: Coping with the burden of "acting white." *Urban Review* 18:176–206.

Freedman, S. W. 1981. Evaluation in the writing conference: An interactive process. In *Selected papers from the 1981 Texas Writing Research Conference,* ed. M. Hairston and C. Selfe, 65–96. Austin: University of Texas at Austin.

_____. 1992. Outside-in and inside-out: Peer response groups in two ninth-grade classes. *Research in the Teaching of English* 26:71–107.

Freedman, S. W., with C. Greenleaf and M. Sperling. 1987. *Response to student writing.* NCTE Research Report no. 23. Urbana, Ill.: National Council of Teachers of English.

Freedman, S. W., and A. Katz. 1987. Pedagogical interaction during th composing process: The writing conference. In *Writing in real time: Model ing production processes,* ed. A. Matsuhashi. Norwood, N.J.: Ablex.

Gere, A. R., and R. D. Abbott. 1985. Talking about writing: The language o writing groups. *Research in the Teaching of English* 19:362-85.

Gere, A. R., and R. Stevens. 1985. The language of writing groups: How ora response shapes revision. In *The acquisition of written language: Respons and revision,* ed. S. W. Freedman, 85-105. Norwood, N.J.: Ablex.

Goetz, J. P., and M. D. LeCompte. 1984. *Ethnography and qualitative desig in educational research.* Orlando, Fla.: Academic Press.

Harris, J. 1989. The idea of community in the study of writing. *College Composition and Communication* 40:11-22.

Hawkins, T. 1980. Intimacy and audience: The relationship between revision and the social dimension of peer tutoring. *College English* 42:64-68.

_____. 1990. A collaborative framework for learning about peer tutoring. Paper presented at the annual convention of the Conference on College Composition and Communication, Chicago, March.

Heath, S. B. 1983. *Ways with words: Language, life, and work in communities and classrooms.* Cambridge: Cambridge University Press.

_____. 1986. Sociocultural contexts of language development. In *Beyond language: Social and cultural factors in schooling language minority students,* 143-86. Los Angeles: California State University, Evaluation, Dissemination and Assessment Center.

Hess, R. D., and V. C. Shipman. 1965. Early experience and the socialization of cognitive modes in children. *Child Development* 36:869-86.

Hull, G., and M. Rose. 1989. Rethinking remediation: Toward a social-cognitive understanding of problematic reading and writing. *Written Communication* 6:139-54.

_____. 1990. Toward a social-cognitive understanding of problematic reading and writing. In *The right to literacy,* ed. A. Lunsford, H. Moglen, and J. Slevin. New York: Modern Language Association.

Hull, G., M. Rose, K. L. Fraser, and M. Castellano. 1991. Remediation as social construct: Perspectives from an analysis of classroom discourse. *College Composition and Communication* 42:299-329.

Hymes, D. H. 1972. Introduction. In *Functions of language in the classroom,* ed. C. B. Cazden, V. P. John, and D. H. Hymes, xi-lvii. New York: Teachers College Press.

_____. 1974. Ways of speaking. In *Explorations in the ethnography of speaking,* ed. R. Bauman and J. Sherzer, 433-51. New York: Cambridge University Press.

Jensen, A. R. 1969. How much can we boost IQ and scholastic achievement? *Harvard Educational Review* 39:1-123.

Jones, R. L. 1989. What's wrong with Black English. In *Viewpoints*, ed. W. R. Adams. Lexington, Mass.: D. C. Heath.

Kaufman, N. S., and G. Dolman. 1984. *Minorities in higher education: The changing Southwest, California.* Boulder, Colo.: Western Interstate Commission for Higher Education.

Kutz, E. 1986. Between students' language and academic discourse: Interlanguage as middle ground. *College English* 48:385-96.

Labov, W. 1972. *Language in the inner city: Studies in the Black English vernacular.* Philadelphia: University of Pennsylvania Press.

_____. 1982. Competing value systems in inner-city schools. In *Children in and out of school: Ethnography and education,* ed. P. Gilmore and A. A. Glatthorn, 148-71. Washington, D.C.: Center for Applied Linguistics.

Lambert, W. 1977. The effects of bilingualism on the individual: Cognitive and sociocultural consequences. In *Bilingualism: Psychological, social and educational implications,* ed. P. A. Hornby, 15-28. New York: Academic Press.

Lamming, G. 1970. *In the castle of my skin.* Ann Arbor: University of Michigan.

McCutcheon, G. 1981. On the interpretation of classroom observations. *Educational Researcher* 10 (5): 5-10.

McLeod, S. 1987. Some thoughts about feelings: The affective domain and the writing process. *College Composition and Communication* 38:426-35.

Magner, D. K. 1990. Black students call for improved access to colleges. *Chronicle of Higher Education* 36 (41): A2.

Maxwell, M. 1990. *When tutor meets student: Experiences in collaborative learning [Nineteen vignettes by peer tutors].* Kensington, Md.: MM Associates.

Mehan, H. 1978. Structuring school structure. *Harvard Educational Review* 48:32-64.

_____. 1979a. *Learning lessons: Social organization in the classroom.* Cambridge, Mass.: Harvard University Press.

_____. 1979b. "What time is it, Denise?": Asking known information questions in classroom discourse. *Theory into Practice* 18:285-94.

_____. 1980. The competent student. *Anthropology and Education Quarterly* 11:131-52.

_____. 1987. Language and schooling. In *Interpretive ethnography of education: At home and abroad,* ed. G. Spindler and L. Spindler, 109-36. Hillsdale, N.J.: Lawrence Erlbaum.

Merriam, S. B. 1988. *Case study research in education: A qualitative approach.* San Francisco: Jossey-Bass.

Meyer, E., and L. Z. Smith. 1987. *The practical tutor.* New York: Oxford University Press.

Monaghan, P. 1990. The long honeymoon of Occidental College's John Slaughter. *Chronicle of Higher Education* 38 (5): A3.

National Commission on Secondary Education for Hispanics. 1984. *Make something happen: Hispanics and urban high school reform.* Washington, D.C.: Hispanic Policy Development Project.

Nystrand, M. 1986. Learning to write by talking about writing: A summary of research on intensive peer review in expository writing instruction at the University of Wisconsin–Madison. In *The structure of written communication: Studies in reciprocity between writers and readers,* ed. M. Nystrand, 179–211. Orlando, Fla.: Academic Press.

Ogbu, J. U. 1974. *The next generation: An ethnography of education in an urban neighborhood.* New York: Academic Press.

———. 1978. *Minority education and caste: The American system in cross-cultural perspective.* New York: Academic Press.

———. 1979. Social stratification and the socialization of competence. *Anthropology and Education Quarterly* 10:3–20.

———. 1982. Cultural discontinuities and schooling. *Anthropology and Education Quarterly* 13:290–307.

———. 1985. Research currents: Cultural-ecological influences on minority school learning. *Language Arts* 62:860–69.

———. 1987. Variability in minority school performance: A problem in search of an explanation. *Anthropology and Education Quarterly* 18:312–34.

Ogbu, J. U., and M. E. Matute-Bianchi. 1986. Understanding sociocultural factors: Knowledge, identity, and school adjustment. In *Beyond language: Social and cultural factors in schooling language minority students,* 73–142. Los Angeles: California State University, Evaluation, Dissemination and Assessment Center.

Patton, M. Q. 1990. *Qualitative evaluation and research methods.* Beverly Hills, Calif.: Sage Publications. Rev. ed. of *Qualitative evaluation methods,* 1980.

Philips, S. U. 1972. Participant structures and communicative competence: Warm Springs children in community and classroom. In *Functions of language in the classroom,* ed. C. B. Cazden, V. P. John, and D. Hymes, 370–94. New York: Teachers College Press.

———. 1982. *The invisible culture: Communication in classroom and community on the Warm Springs Indian Reservation.* New York: Longman.

Rose, M. 1984. *Writer's block: The cognitive dimension.* Carbondale, Ill.: Southern Illinois University Press.

_____. 1989. *Lives on the boundary: The struggles and achievements of America's underprepared.* New York: The Free Press.

Shaughnessy, M. P. 1976. Diving in: An introduction to basic writing. *College Composition and Communication* 27:234–39.

_____. 1977. *Errors and expectations: A guide for the teacher of basic writing.* New York: Oxford University Press.

Severino, C. 1992. Where the cultures of basic writers and academia intersect: Cultivating the common ground. *Journal of Basic Writing* 11:4–15.

Smith, T. W. 1990. *Ethnic images.* Chicago: National Opinion Research Center.

Sperling, M. 1990. I want to talk to each of you: Collaboration and the teacher-student writing conference. *Research in the Teaching of English* 24:279–321.

Sperling, M., and S. W. Freedman. 1987. A good girl writes like a good girl: Written response to student writing. *Written Communication* 4:343–69.

Spradley, J. P. 1980. *Participant observation.* New York: Holt, Rinehart, and Winston.

Valdés, G. 1989. *Identifying priorities in the study of the writing of Hispanic background students* (Grant no. OERI-G-008690004). Washington, D.C.: U.S. Department of Education, Office of Educational Research and Improvement.

_____. 1991. Language issues in writing: The problem of compartmentalization of interest areas within CCCC. Paper presented at the annual convention of the Conference on College Composition and Communication, Boston, March.

Vygotsky, L. S. 1978. *Mind in society: The development of higher psychological processes.* Ed. M. Cole. Cambridge, Mass.: Harvard University Press.

Walker, R. 1980. The conduct of educational case studies: Ethics, theory and procedures. In *Rethinking educational research,* ed. W. B. Dockrell and D. Hamilton. London: Hodder and Stoughton.

Walvoord, B. E., and L. P. McCarthy, with V. J. Anderson. 1991. *Thinking and writing in college: A naturalistic study of students in four disciplines.* Urbana, Ill.: National Council of Teachers of English.

Weiner, S. S. 1990. Accrediting bodies must require a commitment to diversity when measuring a college's quality. *Chronicle of Higher Education* 37 (6): B1, B3.

Werner, H. 1948. *Comparative psychology of mental development.* Chicago: Follett.

Wertsch, J. V. 1991. *Voices of the mind: A sociocultural approach to mediated action.* Cambridge, Mass.: Harvard University Press.

Whiteman, M. 1981. Dialect influence in writing. In *Writing: The nature, development and teaching of written communication,* ed. M. F. Whiteman, vol. 1, *Variation in writing: Functional and linguistic-cultural differences.* Hillsdale, N.J.: Lawrence Erlbaum.

Wilkerson, I. 1989. Beyond the ivory tower. *Fraternity Newsletter* 17 (2): 1, 6.

Williams, W. C. 1963. *Paterson.* New York: New Directions.

Appendix: Interview Questions

Focal Student Interviews

Beginning-of-Term Interviews

- Tell me a bit about your background: Where did you grow up? [For immigrant students: How long have you lived in the United States?] What is your first language? Which language was spoken in your home? [For nonnative speakers: How old were you when you began speaking English?] In which language did you learn to read and write? In what contexts today are you more likely to use your first language? In what contexts are you more likely to use English?

- What are your reasons for attending college? What is your major? What are your career goals?

- What are you hoping to get out of English 90 this semester? Thus far, how would you assess what you're achieving?

- What role is the small-group component playing in helping you toward your goals? How are the small-group sessions different from your regular class? What do you see as the purpose of these sessions? Is there anything in particular that would make them more effective in meeting your needs?

- Do you sometimes find working with classmates on your writing to be useful? Please explain and give some examples.

- How would you describe your relationship with your group leader? For example, would you say that she's more a friend or a teacher, or would you use some other term? Explain.

- What do you think of DPU so far? Do you feel comfortable and at home, that you can "be yourself" here? As an ethnic student, have you faced any special challenges? What's hindered and helped as you've addressed these challenges?

- If I had the power to appoint you DPU President's adviser on equity-student affairs, what would you like to say to him at your first meeting? Do you have any stories to tell about your own experiences that he might find instructive? What do administrators need to know about equity students? What do teachers here—most of whom are accustomed to working with students who are, like themselves, Anglo—need to know in order to work more effectively with equity students? Do group leaders need special preparation to work with equity students? If so, what sorts of preparation?

- If you had unlimited funding, resources, and authority, what sort of adjunct program would you set up? How would you select, train, and supervise group leaders? Would you restructure their role vis-à-vis the basic writing classrooms in any way?

End-of-Term Interviews

- When I asked earlier what you were hoping to get out of English 90 this semester, you said [students' earlier response summarized]. How well have you fulfilled these goals? Would you add anything to your earlier response?

- What role did the small-group component of this class play in helping you toward your goals? How were the small-group sessions different from your regular class? What do you see as the purpose of these sessions? Is there anything in particular that would have made them more effective in meeting your needs? [Where pertinent, students were asked why they did not attend the small groups regularly, and/or why they brought in drafts of writing infrequently.]

- When I asked earlier how you see the difference between small-group sessions and one-on-one tutoring, you said [students' earlier responses reviewed]. Would you like to add to or change that response now?

- Did you sometimes find working with classmates on your writing to be useful? Please explain and give some examples.

- When I asked earlier how you would describe your relationship with your group leader, you said [earlier response reviewed]. How would you now describe your relationship with your group leader?

- When I asked earlier about your progress toward adjusting to DPU, you spoke about [earlier response reviewed]. Would you add anything to that response now—have there been any new challenges, issues, victories, or roadblocks this semester?

- When I asked earlier what you would like to say to DPU's President if appointed his special adviser on equity-student affairs, you said [earlier response reviewed]. Anything you'd now add to that response? What do administrators, teachers, and group leaders need to know about what it's like to be an equity student here at DPU?

(At the conclusion of end-of-term interviews, students were handed transcripts of selected small-group sessions, and the audiotapes of these segments were played back [these same segments were played back to group leaders]. Students were asked for their general response to these episodes, selected because they were particularly representative or key.)

Group Leader Interviews

Beginning-of-Term Interviews

- Please reflect a bit on each of the students with whom you're working this term [this set of questions to be repeated for each student to be discussed]: What would you like to see each accomplish? What will you do to support each student's movement toward these goals?

- What are your priorities in the small groups—what seems most essential, most useful? If students have brought in writing, for example, what's your strategy? If they're brainstorming? If you're working on trouble spots? Does your strategy differ from student to student? If so, how?

- What is your mission with regard to this group of students? (Reflect aloud a bit regarding what your job is and what role/roles you assume, as if describing your work to somebody who does not understand the purpose of the small-group component.) What is the instructor's mission?

- Do you learn from your students? If so, how, why, and what?

- What's different, if anything, about the small-group sessions versus one-on-one tutoring? Do you ever prefer one over the other? If so, why? Do you think students sometimes prefer one or the other?

- How useful or important is it for students to work with one another on their writing? Do you encourage or discourage such peer interaction? If you encourage it, how?

- How would you characterize your students' levels of motivation? Is there anything in particular you do to help encourage and motivate them?

- How would you describe the adjustment that the equity students in this class have to make to this campus, which is mostly white? What problems do they encounter? What kinds of resources do you present? What resources does the classroom teacher present?

- If I had the power to appoint you the college President's adviser on equity-student affairs, what would you like to say to him at your first meeting? What do administrators need to know about equity students? What do teachers here—most of whom are accustomed to working with students who are, like themselves, white—need to know in order to work more effectively with equity students? Do group leaders need special preparation to work with equity students? If so, what sorts of preparation?

- Tell me a bit about your training and experience.

- In general, what do group leaders need to know in order to work effectively with basic writers? If you had unlimited funding, resources, and authority, what sort of adjunct program would you set up—how would you select, train, and supervise the group leaders? Is there any support or training you wish you'd received when you first started out—or you wish you could receive now?

- How do you know when a small-group session has been successful? So far, which of your sessions have been most successful?

End-of-Term Interviews

- Reflect a bit on the progress of each of your students this term [this set of questions to be repeated for each student to be discussed]: What particular roadblocks or issues has this student confronted with regard to writing—or to academic life in general? What are this student's most significant accomplishments? What will be his/her greatest strengths as he/she continues his/her studies? What might hold this student back?
- How would you assess your work with this student this term? What has pleased you most about your work together? What do you wish you had done differently?
- What were the main differences and similarities between what you offered this student and what his/her regular classroom instructor offered? What accounts for these differences and similarities?
- Has your vision of your task—your priorities, goals, attitudes—changed at all this semester? If so, how? If/when you work in the adjunct program again, would you approach your work any differently? If so, how?
- When I asked earlier how you know when a small-group session has been successful, you said [summary of earlier response]. Would you change or add to that response now?
- Have you worked one-on-one this semester? If so, what's been the difference between those sessions and your group work?
- To what extent have your students worked with one another on writing this semester? Do you consider such collaboration among students useful? Explain.
- What difficulties or frustrations have you encountered this term? How did you deal with these? What sorts of training or other support have helped—or conceivably might help?

(At the conclusion of end-of-term interviews, group leaders were handed transcripts of selected sessions, and the audiotapes of these segments were played back [these same segments were discussed with focal students]. Group leaders were asked for their general response to these episodes, selected because they were particularly representative or key.)

Course Instructor Interviews (Susan Williams)

Beginning-of-Term Interview

- Tell me a bit about your professional background—training, experience, aspirations, etc.

- [I read a list of possible focal students from her class, and then asked Williams for her perceptions of each.] Going down the list of these (possible focal) students, tell me a bit about each: How do you perceive this student's level of motivation and ability? What special problems and resources does this student bring to your classroom? What is your vision of what this student needs to accomplish this semester? What will be your role in supporting this process? What will be the group leaders' role? Compare this student to the class as a whole. Is he/she typical of students in this class, or is he/she significantly different?

- How would you define the difference between this class and the writing and reading "skills" course most of your students took last semester?

- How are your basic writing classes different from and similar to the other writing classes you've taught over the years? What do you find particularly problematic about these basic writing classes? What do you find particularly gratifying, exciting, or intriguing? How would you characterize your approach to teaching basic writing as compared to your approach to teaching freshman composition? How is your strategy in the two sorts of classes the same, and how is it different?

- What is your mission with regard to this group of students? What is the group leaders' mission? (How would you explain the difference to someone who doesn't understand why there are both teachers and group leaders?)

- What's different, if anything, about small-group assistance versus one-on-one tutoring?

- Characterize the adjustment the equity students in this class have to make to this campus, which is mostly white. What problems do they encounter? What kinds of resources do you present, and what resources do the group leaders present? Please describe.

- If I had the power to appoint you the college President's adviser on equity-student affairs, what would you like to say to him at your first meeting? What do administrators need to know about equity students? What do teachers here—most of whom are accustomed to working with students who are, like themselves, white—need to know in order to work more effectively with equity students? Do group leaders need special preparation to work with equity students? If so, what sorts of preparation?

- What do group leaders need to know in order to work effectively with basic writers? If you had unlimited funding, resources, and authority, what sort of adjunct program would you set up—how would you select, train, and supervise the group leaders? Would you restructure their role vis-à-vis the basic writing classrooms in any way?

End-of-Term Interview

- Please reflect a bit on the progress of each of the focal students this term [these questions to be repeated for each student to be discussed]:
  - What have been the particular roadblocks and issues this student has confronted? Where has he or she succeeded most notably? What is your assessment of this student's chances for success in freshman composition? What strengths will this student bring with him or her into mainstream academic work, and what weaknesses will he or she still have?
  - How has your class met this student's needs? What role has the adjunct segment played?
  - How do you feel about the group leaders' work with this student this term? Based upon what you've heard and seen of the group leaders' work with this student, what special guidance or training have you offered (or would like to offer) the group leaders? What are the greatest strengths each group leader brings to working with this student, and what does each most need to improve upon?
  - Compare this student to the class as a whole. Is he or she typical of students in this class, or is he or she significantly different?
- Reflect a bit upon this semester's class as a whole. Was it a typical basic writing class, similar to others you've taught, or were there significant differences? Was there anything in particular that struck you about this class, or anything unusual about either the students or the way you approached them?
- How do you feel about small-group assistance? What are the pros and cons of providing at least some one-on-one tutoring?
- Any new thoughts about how you'd set up an ideal adjunct program, given limitless resources?

Adjunct Coordinator and Program Director Interviews

- Tell me about your role in this program. To what extent do you help train or supervise small-group leaders? What kinds of problems do you help resolve?
- What do you see as the central purpose of the adjunct program? Do the group leaders serve essentially the same purpose as the regular class instructor, or is their role somehow different? Do you see their relationships with students as being the same as that of the basic writing teachers or somehow different?

- What do you see as the greatest strength of this program? What is its greatest weakness? Given unlimited funding and resources, what would you like to see happen to improve it?
- What is different or special about the population of students who enroll in the basic writing workshop?
- What do you think group leaders' primary goals should be in their work with basic writers? How might they best achieve these goals?
- Is part of the group leaders' job to encourage or motivate students? If so, how might one effectively go about this?
- What role do you see the group leaders playing in promoting equity students' academic progress?
- What are the essential characteristics of an effective group leader?

Interviews with Other Basic Writing Teachers

- Is there anything unusual about the way you structure the small-group segment of your class?
- To what extent do you supervise the group leaders working with your section? What kinds of guidance or instruction do you give them?
- What do you see as the appropriate role of group leaders? How is their role different from or similar to your own? Summarize for me in a sentence or two what you see as the main purpose of the adjunct program.
- Do you see the group leaders playing a role in promoting the academic progress of equity students on this campus? Explain.
- How are your basic writing classes different from and similar to the other writing classes you've taught over the years? What do you find particularly problematic about these classes? What do you find particularly gratifying, exciting, or intriguing? How is your approach to teaching basic writing different from, say, your approach to teaching freshman composition?
- What do group leaders need to know in order to work effectively with basic writers? Given unlimited funding and resources, what sort of adjunct program would you like to see—in an ideal world, how might staff be selected, trained, and supervised? How might their role be structured vis-à-vis the basic writing classroom?

Index

Author

Anne DiPardo, a former writing teacher, is Assistant Professor of English Education at the University of Iowa. She has written articles and book chapters on a number of instructional issues, including peer response and the place of narrative in composition curricula. She was named a 1992 NCTE Promising Researcher for work related to this book. Her current research focuses upon teacher development and the institutional contexts of teaching.

Titles in the NCTE Research Report Series

NCTE began publishing the Research Report series in 1963 with *The Language of Elementary School Children.* Volumes 4–6, 8–12, 14, 17, 20, and 21 are out of print. The following titles are available through the NCTE *Catalog.*

Vol. Author and Title

1 Walter D. Loban, *The Language of Elementary School Children* (1963)

2 James R. Squire, *The Responses of Adolescents While Reading Four Short Stories* (1964)

3 Kellogg W. Hunt, *Grammatical Structures Written at Three Grade Levels* (1965)

7 James R. Wilson, *Responses of College Freshmen to Three Novels* (1966)

13 Janet Emig, *The Composing Processes of Twelfth Graders* (1971)

15 Frank O'Hare, *Sentence Combining: Improving Student Writing without Formal Grammar Instruction* (1973)

16 Ann Terry, *Children's Poetry Preferences: A National Survey of Upper Elementary Grades* (1974)

18 Walter Loban, *Language Development: Kindergarten through Grade 12* (1976)

19 F. André Favat, *Child and Tale: The Origins of Interest* (1977)

22 Judith A. Langer and Arthur N. Applebee, *How Writing Shapes Thinking: A Study of Teaching and Learning* (1987)

23 Sarah Warshauer Freedman, *Response to Student Writing* (1987)

24 Anne DiPardo, *A Kind of Passport: A Basic Writing Adjunct Program and the Challenge of Student Diversity* (1993)

25 Arthur N. Applebee, *Literature in the Secondary School: Studies of Curriculum and Instruction in the United States* (1993)

26 Carol D. Lee, *Signifying as a Scaffold for Literary Interpretation: The Pedagogical Implications of an African American Discourse Genre* (1993)